FORWARD TO RICHMOND

McClellan's Peninsular Campaign

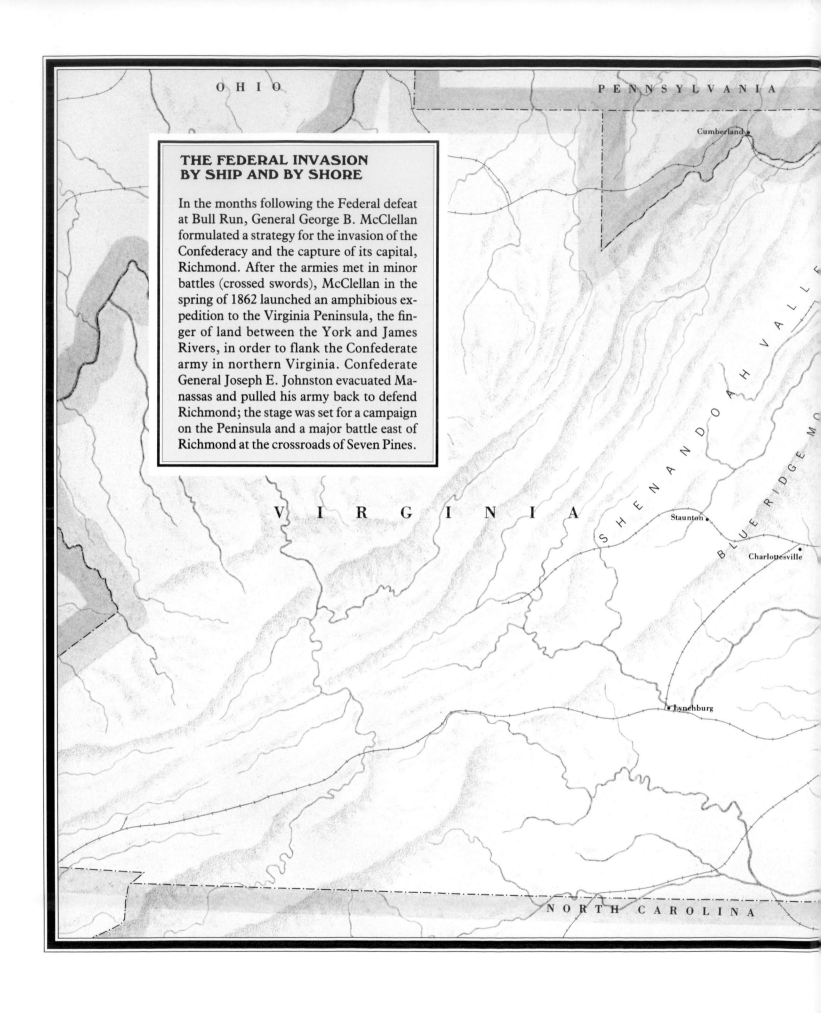

OHIO

PENNSYLVANIA

Cumberland•

THE FEDERAL INVASION
BY SHIP AND BY SHORE

In the months following the Federal defeat
at Bull Run, General George B. McClellan
formulated a strategy for the invasion of the
Confederacy and the capture of its capital,
Richmond. After the armies met in minor
battles (crossed swords), McClellan in the
spring of 1862 launched an amphibious expedition to the Virginia Peninsula, the fin-
ger of land between the York and James
Rivers, in order to flank the Confederate
army in northern Virginia. Confederate
General Joseph E. Johnston evacuated Manassas and pulled his army back to defend
Richmond; the stage was set for a campaign
on the Peninsula and a major battle east of
Richmond at the crossroads of Seven Pines.

VIRGINIA

SHENANDOAH VALLE

BLUE RIDGE MO

Staunton•

Charlottesville•

•Lynchburg

NORTH CAROLINA

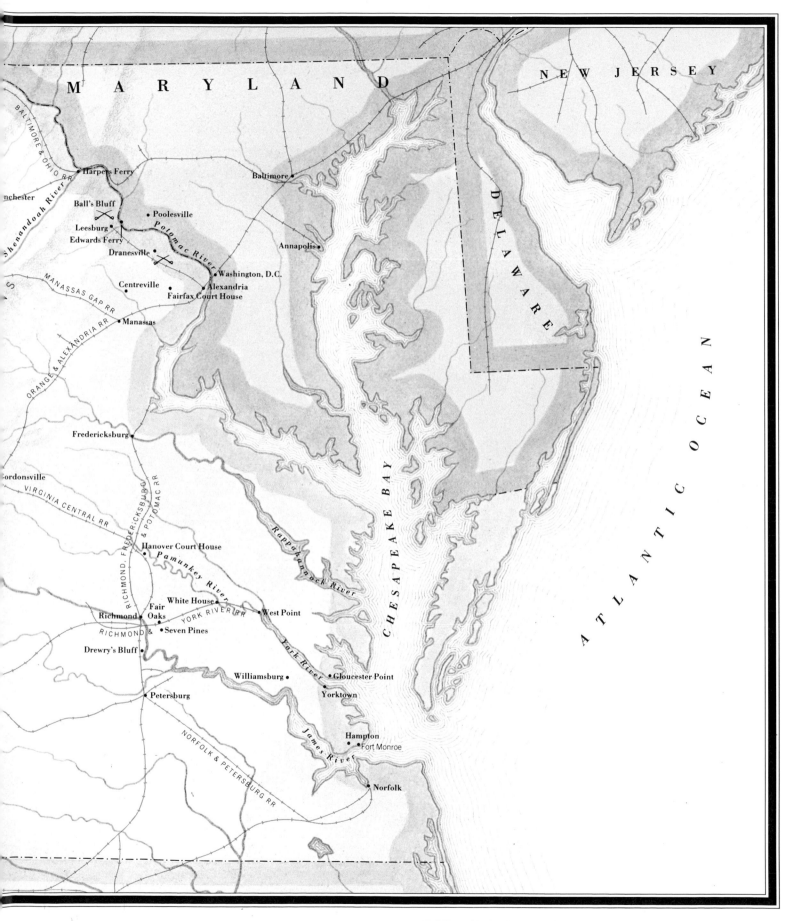

MARYLAND

NEW JERSEY

DELAWARE

BALTIMORE & OHIO RR

Shenandoah River

Winchester

Harpers Ferry

Ball's Bluff

Leesburg

Edwards Ferry

Dranesville

Poolesville

Potomac River

Baltimore

Annapolis

MANASSAS GAP RR

Centreville

Washington, D.C.

Alexandria

Fairfax Court House

ORANGE & ALEXANDRIA RR

Manassas

Fredericksburg

Gordonsville

VIRGINIA CENTRAL RR

RICHMOND, FREDERICKSBURG & POTOMAC RR

Hanover Court House

Pamunkey River

Rappahannock River

CHESAPEAKE BAY

ATLANTIC OCEAN

White House

Fair Oaks

Richmond

Seven Pines

YORK RIVER RR

West Point

RICHMOND &

Drewry's Bluff

York River

Williamsburg

Gloucester Point

Yorktown

Petersburg

NORFOLK & PETERSBURG RR

James River

Hampton

Fort Monroe

Norfolk

Scale of Miles

0   25   50   100

This volume is one of a series that chronicles in full the
events of the American Civil War, 1861-1865.
Other books in the series include:
Brother against Brother: The War Begins
First Blood: Fort Sumter to Bull Run
The Blockade: Runners and Raiders
The Road to Shiloh: Early Battles in the West
Decoying the Yanks: Jackson's Valley Campaign
Confederate Ordeal: The Southern Home Front
Lee Takes Command: From Seven Days to Second Bull Run
The Coastal War: Chesapeake Bay to Rio Grande
Tenting Tonight: The Soldier's Life
The Bloodiest Day: The Battle of Antietam
War on the Mississippi: Grant's Vicksburg Campaign
Rebels Resurgent: Fredericksburg to Chancellorsville
Twenty Million Yankees: The Northern Home Front
Gettysburg: The Confederate High Tide
The Struggle for Tennessee: Tupelo to Stones River
The Fight for Chattanooga: Chickamauga to Missionary Ridge
Spies, Scouts and Raiders: Irregular Operations
The Battles for Atlanta: Sherman Moves East
The Killing Ground: Wilderness to Cold Harbor
Sherman's March: Atlanta to the Sea
Death in the Trenches: Grant at Petersburg
War on the Frontier: The Trans-Mississippi West
The Shenandoah in Flames: The Valley Campaign of 1864
Pursuit to Appomattox: The Last Battles
The Assassination: The Death of the President
The Nation Reunited: War's Aftermath
Master Index: An Illustrated Guide

The Cover: As the bugler sounds the command, a
battery of the 5th U.S. Artillery in General George B.
McClellan's Army of the Potomac prepares to
deploy along a line marked by the flag-bearer. The
best-trained branch of the Federal Army, the
artillery earned a fearsome reputation among the
Confederates during the Peninsular Campaign.

THE
CIVIL
WAR

FORWARD TO RICHMOND

BY

RONALD H. BAILEY

AND THE

EDITORS OF TIME-LIFE BOOKS

McClellan's Peninsular Campaign

TIME-LIFE BOOKS, ALEXANDRIA, VIRGINIA

Time-Life Books Inc.
is a wholly owned subsidiary of
TIME INCORPORATED

FOUNDER: Henry R. Luce 1898-1967

Editor-in-Chief: Henry Anatole Grunwald
President: J. Richard Munro
Chairman of the Board: Ralph P. Davidson
Corporate Editor: Jason McManus
Group Vice President, Books: Joan D. Manley

TIME-LIFE BOOKS INC.

EDITOR: George Constable
Executive Editor: George Daniels
Director of Design: Louis Klein
Editorial Board: Roberta R. Conlan, Ellen Phillips,
Gerry Schremp, Gerald Simons, Rosalind Stubenberg,
Kit van Tulleken
Editorial General Manager: Neal Goff
Director of Research: Phyllis K. Wise
Director of Photography: John Conrad Weiser

PRESIDENT: Reginald K. Brack Jr.
Senior Vice President: William Henry
Vice Presidents: George Artandi, Stephen L. Bair,
Robert A. Ellis, Juanita T. James, Christopher T. Linen,
James L. Mercer, Joanne A. Pello, Paul R. Stewart

The Civil War
Editor: Gerald Simons
Deputy Editor: Henry Woodhead
Designer: Herbert H. Quarmby
Chief Researcher: Philip Brandt George

Editorial Staff for *Forward to Richmond*
Associate Editor: Sara Schneidman (pictures)
Staff Writers: Adrienne George, David Johnson,
Glenn McNatt, John Newton
Researchers: Brian C. Pohanka (principal);
Harris J. Andrews, Gwen C. Mullen
Assistant Designer: Cynthia T. Richardson
Copy Coordinators: Stephen G. Hyslop,
Anthony K. Pordes
Picture Coordinator: Donna Quaresima
Editorial Assistants: Andrea E. Reynolds,
Annette T. Wilkerson
Special Contributors: Rachel Cox, Jerry Korn

Editorial Operations
Design: Ellen Robling (assistant director)
Copy Room: Diane Ullius
Production: Anne B. Landry (director), Celia Beattie
Quality Control: James J. Cox (director), Sally Collins
Library: Louise D. Forstall

Correspondents: Elisabeth Kraemer-Singh (Bonn);
Margot Hapgood, Dorothy Bacon (London); Miriam
Hsia (New York); Maria Vincenza Aloisi, Josephine du
Brusle (Paris); Ann Natanson (Rome).

The Author:
Ronald H. Bailey is a freelance author and journalist who
has written on a variety of subjects for Time-Life Books.
He is the author of *Violence and Aggression* in the Human
Behavior series; *Partisans and Guerrillas, Prisoners of War*
and several other volumes in the World War II series;
and *Glacier* in the Planet Earth series. He has also published several articles on prison reform in *Corrections* magazine. While a senior editor at *Life*, he edited a book of
Larry Burrows' photographs, *Larry Burrows: Compassion-
ate Photographer*.

The Consultants:
Colonel John R. Elting, USA (Ret.), a former Associate
Professor at West Point, is the author of *Battles for Scandi-
navia* in the Time-Life Books World War II series and of
*The Battle of Bunker's Hill, The Battles of Saratoga, Mili-
tary History and Atlas of the Napoleonic Wars* and *American
Army Life*. He is also editor of the three volumes of *Military Uniforms in America, 1755-1867*, and associate editor
of *The West Point Atlas of American Wars*.

James I. Robertson Jr. is C. P. Miles Professor of History
at Virginia Tech. The recipient of the Nevins-Freeman
Award and other prizes in the field of Civil War history, he
has written or edited some 20 books, which include *The
Stonewall Brigade, Civil War Books: A Critical Bibliography* and *Civil War Sites in Virginia*.

William A. Frassanito, a Civil War historian and lecturer
specializing in photograph analysis, is the author of two
award-winning studies, *Gettysburg: A Journey in Time* and
*Antietam: The Photographic Legacy of America's Bloodiest
Day*, and a companion volume, *Grant and Lee, The Virginia Campaigns*. He has also served as chief consultant to the
photographic history series *The Image of War*.

Les Jensen, Curator of the U.S. Army Transportation
Museum at Fort Eustis, Virginia, specializes in Civil War
artifacts and is a conservator of historic flags. He is a
contributor to *The Image of War* series, a freelance writer
and consultant for numerous Civil War publications and
museums, and a member of the Company of Military Historians. He was formerly Curator of the Museum of the
Confederacy in Richmond, Virginia.

Michael McAfee specializes in military uniforms and has
been Curator of Uniforms and History at the West Point
Museum since 1970. A fellow of the Company of Military
Historians, he coedited with Colonel John Elting *Long
Endure: The Civil War Years*, and he collaborated with
Frederick Todd on *American Military Equipage*. He has
written numerous articles for *Military Images Magazine*,
as well as *Artillery of the American Revolution, 1775-1783*.

Library of Congress Cataloguing in Publication Data
Bailey, Ronald H.
  Forward to Richmond
  (The Civil War)
  Bibliography: p.
  Includes index.
  1. Peninsular Campaign, 1862. 1. Time-Life Books.
II. Title. III. Series.
E473.6.B19 1983   973.7'32   83-5034
ISBN 0-8094-4720-7
ISBN 0-8094-4721-5 (lib. bdg.)

CONTENTS

A Young Napoleon

"The true course in conducting military operations is to make no movement until the preparations are as complete as circumstances will permit and never to fight a battle without some definite object worth the probable loss; such a course will ever insure the greatest economy of life, time and treasure, as well as the most decisive results."

MAJOR GENERAL GEORGE B. MCCLELLAN, U.S. ARMY

1

The message that was handed to George Brinton McClellan that summer day came from the President of the United States, and its tone was urgent. "Circumstances make your presence here necessary," it read. "Come hither without delay."

The young general received the summons at his field headquarters in northwestern Virginia, 150 miles from Washington, and he wasted no time in responding. He hurried on horseback to the nearest railroad station and boarded a train on the Baltimore & Ohio line. He arrived at the depot in Washington late on the afternoon of Friday, July 26, 1861.

As McClellan rode down Pennsylvania Avenue in a carriage, he saw many signs of the "circumstances" that required his presence. Five days had passed since the Federal troops routed at Bull Run began pouring into Washington. In spite of the best efforts of General in Chief Winfield Scott to restore order, the capital was still in disarray. Drunken soldiers roamed the streets. Demoralized officers filled the saloons at Willard's and the other fashionable hotels. Frightened civilians braced for the worst. The Confederate victors of Bull Run were now encamped at Centreville, Virginia, scarcely 25 miles southwest of Washington, and many Northerners feared that the enemy was preparing for an all-out assault on the capital.

The morning after his arrival, McClellan went to the White House to find out what the President had in mind for him. It was an assignment that might have shaken a less self-confident man. McClellan was to take command of all Federal troops in and about Washington. He was to ensure the safety of the city and then forge a new army to march on Richmond, Virginia, which had recently replaced Montgomery, Alabama, as the Confederate capital.

That afternoon, the general made a quick tour of the camps on the outskirts of Washington, and he returned with a wholesome respect for his new task. Some fortifications were in place on the far side of the Potomac, where the Federals still controlled the narrow strip of Virginia running north from Alexandria to a point just above and opposite Georgetown. But McClellan noted with dismay that the approaches to Washington on the Maryland side were inadequately guarded.

Furthermore, he had no confidence in the ability of his new command to put up a good fight. Though on paper the army consisted of 51,000 men, only about two thirds of them were available for duty—and for the most part they were ill led and ill trained. "I found no army to command," McClellan wrote later; he had "a mere collection of regiments cowering on the banks of the Potomac, some perfectly raw, others dispirited

Major General George McClellan, called to Washington in July of 1861, said confidently: "God will give me the strength and wisdom to preserve this great nation."

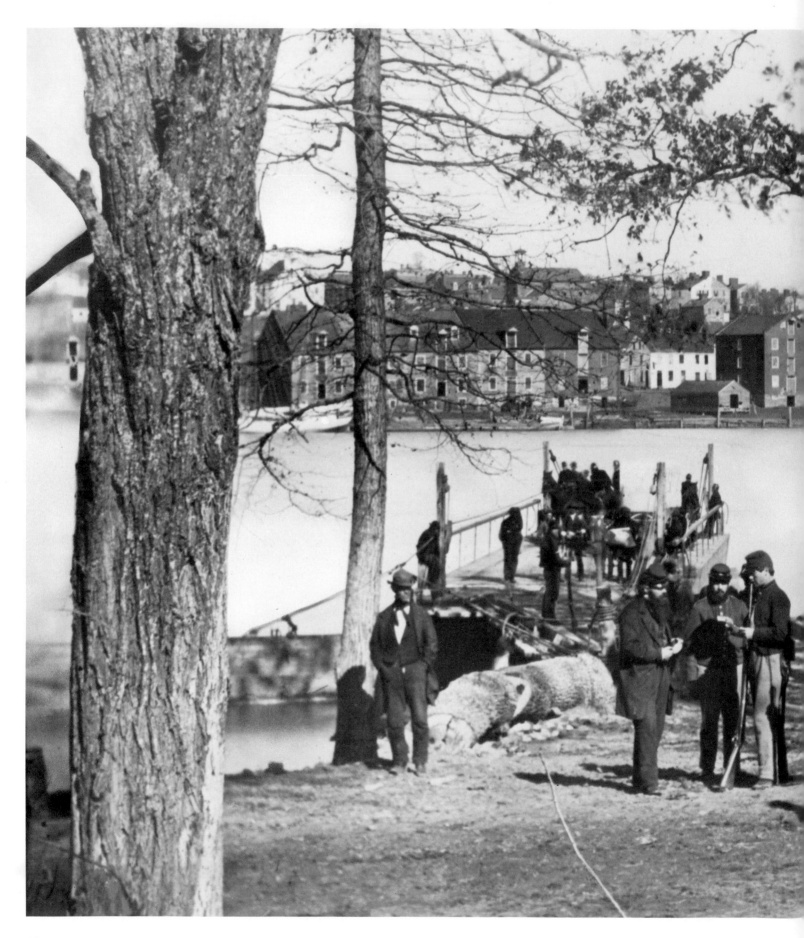

by the recent defeat. The city was almost in condition to have been taken by a dash of a regiment of cavalry."

The capital was in fact vulnerable, though in no real danger. Thus far the Confederates lacked the organization and equipment for a sustained offensive. Still, McClellan's alarmed view was the prevailing one. Horace Greeley, the nervous editor of the New York *Tribune,* said he was so worried that he could not sleep. In the days before Bull Run, Greeley had affixed to his paper's masthead the rousing slogan "Forward to Richmond!" Now the slogan was gone, and so, temporarily, was Greeley's fervor for war. Soon he would write to the President suggesting that the Union make peace with the Confederacy.

These critical times fairly cried out for a hero, and the new general seemed perfectly cast in the role. McClellan was a handsome, charming man with steady gray eyes, a sandy mustache, just the hint of a goatee, and a head of thick, close-cropped auburn hair. He had unmistakable parade-ground dash and glamor. He wore a jaunty French-style kepi, was an excellent horseman and rode a magnificent dark bay by the name of Dan Webster, 17 hands high—the same height as its rider. Though his soldiers referred to him as Little Mac, McClellan was not really short. He was five feet eight inches tall, only a quarter of an inch under the average height for Federal soldiers. But he was built so sturdily—with broad shoulders and a massive chest measuring 45 inches around— that he appeared shorter than he was. Not yet 35 years old, the general radiated what one of his contemporaries called "an indescribable air of success."

Success had come early and often in his

young life. The studious son of a prominent Philadelphia surgeon, McClellan had entered West Point at the age of 15 and graduated second in a class of 59 cadets. As a second lieutenant of engineers, he had distinguished himself in the Mexican War in 1847, winning brevets as first lieutenant and captain for bravery under fire. After stints as an engineering instructor at West Point and as an explorer in various expeditions to the Far West, he was selected in 1855 to serve as a member of a commission studying European armies. Back home after nearly a year abroad, he wrote a book-length analysis of the organization and tactics of foreign armies.

In 1857, McClellan resigned his captain's commission to become chief engineer of the Illinois Central Railroad. Rewards came as readily to him in civilian life as in the military. He was soon promoted to vice president of the Illinois Central and, in May 1860, married a beautiful and vivacious young woman, Ellen "Nellie" Marcy, the daughter of Captain Randolph B. Marcy, McClellan's commander on one of the Western explorations. Four months later McClellan was named president of the Ohio and Mississippi Railroad's Eastern Division, with offices in Cincinnati.

McClellan sensed that war was coming. When he leased a house in Cincinnati for three years, he insisted upon a clause releasing him in the event of hostilities. On April 23, 1861, eleven days after Confederate forces fired on Fort Sumter, he accepted a commission as major general of Ohio volunteers. Soon the War Department gave him command of the Department of Ohio, embracing volunteer forces from Ohio, Indiana and Illinois.

From the outset it was clear that this general was a man with style. He brought his own printing press into the field and used it to issue flamboyant proclamations to his troops. "Soldiers!" he declared in one of these messages, "I have heard there was danger here. I have come to place myself at your head and to share it with you. I fear now but one thing—that you will not find foemen worthy of your steel." His soldiers loved it.

In June, a few weeks before the Federal defeat at Bull Run, George McClellan sent his 20,000 troops across the Ohio River into the western part of Virginia. He had two objectives: to prevent Confederate forces from severing the Baltimore & Ohio Railroad, Washington's direct link with the West; and to preserve for the Union this antisecessionist section of Virginia.

He would succeed on both counts. With three times as many men as his foe, he sent his troops into a series of clashes that routed the Confederates and paved the way for the region's entry into the Union two years later as the new state of West Virginia. These were not major battles, and casualties on both sides were light. But with the exception of Brigadier General Nathaniel Lyon's small victories in Missouri, they were the only Federal successes on the battlefield during the first months of the War. So McClellan was immoderately celebrated in the Northern press, and when he was summoned east, reporters awarded him the romantic title "Young Napoleon."

Yet beneath McClellan's winning ways, vague signs of trouble had appeared. A few officers who served with him in western Virginia claimed that during one battle, at Rich Mountain, he had lacked aggressiveness, even though his subordinate, Brigadier General William S. Rosecrans, had won a smashing victory there. Whatever the merits of that particular charge, others much like it would surface to haunt McClellan again and again.

Friends and associates of the general also noted puzzling contradictions between the public figure and the private man. For example, Brigadier General Jacob Cox, who campaigned with McClellan in western Virginia, reported that McClellan's proclamations with "their turgid rhetoric and exaggerated pretense did not seem natural to him. In them he seemed to be composing for stage effect something to be spoken in character by a quite different person from the sensible and genial man we knew in daily life and conversation."

McClellan raised further questions by regarding his new job with a mixture of arrogance and dedication. The post was not merely an assignment to him but a mission, a sacred trust, an almost divine calling. More and more in the days to come he would feel that he alone could rebuild the army and save the nation, and he would imagine that anyone who opposed his plans or questioned his judgment was his enemy.

Not that McClellan lacked for real en-

A Federal soldier, guilty of breaking Army regulations, is paraded through the streets of Washington. In this ceremonious humiliation, the guards in front carry their guns upside down and the fifer and drummer play the "Rogue's March." Afterward, miscreants were cashiered from the service or sent to the guardhouse.

emies. The importance of his assignment made him a natural target for the capital's politicians; he came to know all too well the dark underside of the Lincoln administration and everywhere encountered men too shrewd and ruthless for a naïve young general. Increasingly McClellan was to turn away in disillusionment and disgust from his own government and even from the President who appointed him and who persisted in protecting him.

McClellan was fated to become a figure of fierce controversy, beloved by his troops, hated and distrusted by sundry opponents, often condemned and written off by the fickle Northern press. Despite the attacks from all quarters, he would remain the most important Federal general in the East for well over a year. In his first nine months of command, he would rebuild the army, restore morale, launch an enormous amphibious assault on the Virginia Peninsula, and campaign through mud and storm, siege and skirmish, to the very gates of Richmond. There, in a boggy wilderness between Seven Pines and Fair Oaks, two great armies would lock in a sprawling two-day battle. This struggle was to prove the first true bloodbath in the East, just as Shiloh had in the West, ushering in clashes of a new and frightening ferocity.

As the man of the hour, with all Washington at his feet, General McClellan plunged into his new assignment with supreme self-assurance. "By some strange operation of magic I seem to have become the power of the land," McClellan confided in a letter to his wife on the day after his arrival. "I see already the main causes of our recent failure; I am sure that I can remedy these, and am

A Grand Tour to Study the Art of War

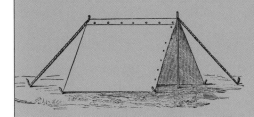

The French *tente d'abri* was adopted by the U.S. Army at McClellan's suggestion. Known to generations of soldiers as the "pup tent," it was easy to assemble and to pack.

A French manual, translated by McClellan in 1852, became the bible for bayonet drills taught to American soldiers. The parries illustrated here were intended to protect the head against saber blows.

In April 1855, Captain George B. McClellan was sent to Europe as a member of a three-man commission to study foreign armies, with a view to improving military organization at home. This was a signal honor for the 28-year-old officer; both his colleagues had graduated from West Point before he was born and were well-known experts in engineering and ordnance. For a year, the commissioners inspected six European armies and hobnobbed with high officials and heads of state. Then they produced their reports.

Of the three, young McClellan's report drew the most attention. It recommended the latest European advances in tactics, equipment and organization. It urged that U.S. cavalrymen be prepared to fight dismounted to provide more accurate firepower. It advocated the establishment of military veterinary and blacksmith schools to prevent the waste of Army horses and mules. And for the common soldier, McClellan advocated lighter and looser clothing, a physical-fitness program and even a new rank—private first class—to reward those men who would do most of the fighting. All in all, McClellan's report cemented his reputation as a promising young officer and did much to increase the efficiency of the U.S. Army.

Captain McClellan *(right)* and his seated colleagues, Majors Alfred Mordecai and Richard Delafield, meet with a high Russian officer, probably in Warsaw.

confident that I can lead these armies of men to victory once more."

The general immediately got down to business. First, to restore rudimentary discipline to the ranks, McClellan appointed as his provost marshal Brigadier General Andrew Porter, who had been an efficient brigade commander at Bull Run, and placed under him more than 1,000 tough and seasoned Regular Army men to serve temporarily as military police.

This new provost guard swarmed through the city's brothels and gambling houses, saloons and hotel lobbies. They enforced the act of Congress that prohibited the sale of liquor to soldiers; they barred civilians from visiting camps without special permission; and they arrested anyone in Federal blue—officer or enlisted man—who lacked written authorization to be away from his post. The new broom swept clean. By the close of the first week in August, less than two weeks after McClellan took command, practically all of the errant soldiers were in jail or back on duty.

That was only the first step in restoring discipline. Men in several local camps were threatening mutiny. These soldiers had volunteered to serve three years with their regiments, but they grew restless watching other volunteers going home. The departing recruits had answered President Lincoln's first call in mid-April for three-month volunteers, and they were being mustered out by their state militia units now that their terms of enlistment had been served.

McClellan cracked down hard on the mutinous three-year men. When the 2nd Maine Infantry refused to turn out one morning, he dispatched the provost guard to arrest the ringleaders. Soon 63 soldiers were on their way to Fort Jefferson, a military prison in the Dry Tortugas, off the southern tip of Florida.

The strongest test of McClellan's new discipline came from the 79th New York Highlanders. The Highlanders had suffered frightfully at Bull Run, losing one fourth of the regiment—including their colonel, James Cameron, brother of the Secretary of War. The regimental historian wrote that after the battle, " 'I want to go home' was pictured on every countenance."

Then a misunderstanding arose. The soldiers of the 79th were somehow led to believe that they would be allowed leave to return home to New York City for the purpose of recruiting new volunteers to fill their depleted ranks. When the Highlanders learned that they would not be going home after all, a number of them got drunk and worked up a nasty temper. The next morning, the 14th of August, all but two of the regiment's 10 companies refused orders to strike their tents in preparation for a march to another camp.

As soon as McClellan got wind of the trouble, he sent Provost Marshal Porter and a heavily armed guard of several hundred regulars to surround the regiment. On a hill overlooking the camp, Regular Army artillerymen loaded their pieces with canister, a charge of lead balls. That sufficed to end the uprising. The mutineers were disarmed, and 35 ringleaders were placed in irons and hauled off to the guardhouse.

McClellan dealt out a heavier blow to the regiment's pride: He ordered the provost marshal to strip the 79th of its regimental colors. An officer of the provost guard remembered later that when the regimental flags were taken away from the camp, there emerged "a low cry like a protesting moan from those nearest the colors."

In making an example of the Highlanders, McClellan was at the same time priming them for rehabilitation. He announced that the regimental colors would be restored to the Highlanders when they gave evidence that they had learned to behave like soldiers. True to his word, he personally returned the colors to the regiment about a month later, after the Highlanders had demonstrated good discipline under fire on a minor reconnaissance mission across the Potomac in Virginia. "We cheered him heartily," a Highlander wrote, "feeling that Little Mac was, after all, our friend."

McClellan spent most of his time organizing, building and training the army. To oversee the multitudinous tasks required of his command, he put together a large staff. His appointments included a chief of artillery to expand a badly neglected force that started out with only nine batteries and 30 guns, a medical director to establish hospitals and to show regimental officers how to lay out a camp with better sanitation, and a quartermaster general to supply the needs of soldiers—who wore out a new pair of shoes in just two months and a new uniform in four months. Eventually the general's staff numbered 65 officers.

Then, seeking to coordinate the duties of his burgeoning staff, McClellan created a post common among European armed forces but new to the United States Army: chief of staff. The officer he named to the post was his father-in-law, Randolph Marcy, who by now had risen to the rank of colonel.

Of special importance to McClellan's methodical engineer's mind was the construction of fortifications around Washington. He immediately endorsed plans already under way for a series of 48 forts and redoubts to guard the city's 37-mile perimeter. When completed, the Virginia defenses would extend north from Alexandria to the Chain Bridge across the Potomac above Georgetown, and the Maryland defenses would flank Washington at distances of up to eight miles from the city.

While these new fortifications were taking shape, McClellan fretted constantly about the safety of the capital. Early in August, the Confederates under Brigadier General Joseph E. Johnston—an old comrade of McClellan's from the Mexican War—edged closer to Washington, occupying Fairfax Court House, about 15 miles west of the city. McClellan, anticipating an attack at any time, wrote his wife on the 8th of August, "I have scarcely slept one moment for the last three nights knowing well that the enemy intend some movement and fully recognizing our own weakness."

McClellan worried not only about the proximity of Johnston's army but also about its size, which he constantly exaggerated. He told his wife "the enemy have from three to four times my force." Actually, Johnston had fewer than 40,000 men available for duty during most of August, while the rapidly growing Federal forces numbered nearly 70,000. Indeed, Johnston had no intention of attacking Washington unless he received substantial reinforcements from Richmond; the Battle of Bull Run had left him short of fresh troops, food and ammunition. "Our army was more disorganized by victory," he claimed later, "than that of the United States by defeat."

By September, McClellan felt he could breathe somewhat more easily. Discipline had been restored and construction of the fortifications around Washington was well enough along that he deemed the capital safe from any immediate danger. Now the general could devote full attention to the third and most formidable of his tasks: forging an army strong enough to take the offensive and to capture Richmond.

His army already was new in name. What had previously been called the Division of the Potomac was rechristened the Army of the Potomac on August 20. It comprised not only the troops in and around Washington but also those posted in all of Maryland and Delaware, and in the Shenandoah Valley near Harpers Ferry, Virginia, about 50 miles upriver from the capital.

The army was also largely new in composition. The three-month militia units, which had formed the bulk of the Federal forces at Bull Run, had gone home. They were replaced by new recruits, enlisting for three years in answer to President Lincoln's call in July for 500,000 volunteers. These fresh troops were pouring in as rapidly as the railroads could handle them. Recruited in regiments in their home states, they reached Washington at the rate of 10,000 men a week during August and September.

The recruits were stationed temporarily at the new encampments springing up on the outskirts of Washington, each laid out according to regulations in orderly company streets. In these camps the troops were issued equipment, introduced to soldierly discipline and, as Private Alfred Bellard of the 5th New Jersey Infantry reported in his diary, "initiated in the misteries of keeping our heels on a line. Toes out at an angle of 45 degrees. Belly in. Chest out and such other positions as tend to make a

Flanked by large signal flags, Pennsylvania volunteers take time out from a training course in the newly formed Signal Corps. They practiced their mysterious wigwags, a kind of semaphore, on Red Hill above Georgetown, to the fascination of observers for miles around.

full fledged veteran out of a raw recruit."

After being drilled in correct posture, the men were taught marching movements—how to about-face and make turns at command. They were then given weapons, tutored in the manual of arms and marched about with the full accouterments. Companies learned to move swiftly from column to line of battle and back again, and to face an attack coming from any direction. Once mastered, these maneuvers were then performed at a faster pace, either quick time or double-quick time.

Bayonet drill was not neglected; McClellan himself had formulated the Army's drill in that weapon with liberal borrowings from a French text. The thrusts and parries involved in bayonet training resembled those of fencing, and the exercise was useful in improving the soldier's coordination and reflexes. Target practice was uncommon, however; it appeared to be of minor importance since massed firepower, not individual marksmanship, was the basis of established infantry tactics.

After a few weeks of this basic training, most regiments moved across the Potomac to join the somewhat more seasoned units already encamped on the Virginia side, and to receive further instruction. There, McClellan shaped the organization of his new army. The men were drilled to maneuver proficiently in progressively larger units. The 10 companies of each infantry regiment learned to march together, and then the several regiments that formed a brigade were united in drill. Finally, divisions were assembled, each ordinarily consisting of three brigades of infantry, one regiment of cavalry and four batteries of artillery. The customary strength of a division was 10,000 men,

An actual sketch, made on the spot by one of the Special Artists of Frank Leslie's Illustrated Newspaper.

Mr. Leslie holds the copyright and reserves the exclusive right of publication.

though in actual practice it was anywhere from 7,000 to 12,000.

To command his new divisions, McClellan called on the services of experienced regulars, almost all of them West Pointers and many of them old comrades from the prewar Army. But finding competent officers below the divisional level proved to be one of McClellan's most vexing problems. Many of the present regimental commanders owed their rank to political influence; they had been appointed by the governor of their state or, in some cases, elected by their units, with little regard for military experience or competence.

Typical of the unqualified officers was an elderly company commander from New England whose men arrived in Washington with rusty rifles; he had not realized that

A 300-foot rubber pontoon bridge across the Anacostia River is tested by the 15th New York Engineers under the appreciative gaze of visiting dignitaries (*bottom right*). The experimental span was flung together in 20 minutes by 200 engineers as a graduation exercise after a month of intensive training.

Washington joke, a boy who threw a stone at a dog on Pennsylvania Avenue missed the cur, but hit three new brigadiers.

Among the best of the new lot—and undoubtedly the most colorful—was Philip Kearny, a millionaire adventurer and socialite who had fought with the French Chasseurs d'Afrique, a crack light cavalry outfit, in Algeria in 1840. Kearny was living in Paris when the Civil War broke out, and returned to join up. He had two handicaps: First, in an Army dominated by West Point graduates, he had not attended the academy, and second, he had only one arm. As a young dragoon captain in the Mexican War, Kearny had remarked in a burst of youthful enthusiasm that he would give an arm to lead a charge against the enemy. A few days later, at Churubusco, he got his wish and paid the price.

The loss of an arm had not stopped Kearny from fighting. He served in 1859 with the French Army of Napoleon III against the Austrians. Swinging a saber and clenching his horse's reins between his teeth, he had led charges with such valor that he was awarded the Legion of Honor. When Kearny received his Federal commission in 1861 and took command of the New Jersey Brigade early in August, he had probably seen more battle than any other general in the Army of the Potomac.

On Kearny's first encounter with his brigade, he was wearing civilian clothes—his new uniform was still at the tailors—and no one recognized him as the new general. Under the stump of his left arm he carried a walking stick, and it immediately came in handy. Near the camp's unguarded gate he saw a cluster of officers passing around a bottle of whiskey. Waxing so angry "you

the weapons had to be cleaned and oiled regularly. "The officers, with but very few exceptions," complained Brigadier General George Meade, an irritable West Point graduate who commanded one of the Pennsylvania brigades, "are ignorant, inefficient and worthless."

To weed out unfit officers, McClellan made extensive use of the new selection boards that Congress had recently authorized. Many officers resigned rather than face examination by the exacting Army officers who sat on the boards. Within eight months 310 officers had either yielded their place or had been cashiered.

Meanwhile, to command the dozens of brigades being organized by McClellan, the President was commissioning so many new brigadier generals that, according to one could practically see the smoke rising out of him,'' remembered a witness, Kearny smashed the bottle with a sweep of the stick. Thereafter, he set about shaping up his brigade by working his men hard and the officers even harder. Soon a New Jersey soldier could report with pride, "He's the top Brigadier in the whole army." The soldier added thoughtfully: "And if he ain't, at least he's the richest."

In the Army of the Potomac that late summer and early fall of 1861, no one worked harder than the young general his troops called Little Mac or Our George. It was not uncommon for McClellan to spend 12 hours or more a day in the saddle, inspecting the sprawling cities of white-tented camps that now surrounded Washington. He wanted "to see as much as I can every day," he wrote his wife, "and, more than that, to let the men see me and gain confidence in me."

McClellan was sure to be seen, for every visit from the general was an event, his mere passage down the street an exciting cavalcade. First came McClellan himself, posting smoothly at a fast trot on his big bay. Stretched behind the general, struggling to keep up with his horse's long-legged gait, trotted a cavalry escort and a large retinue of aides-de-camp.

McClellan maintained a personal staff that at one time numbered no fewer than 19 aides. One of them was even wealthier than Philip Kearny—John Jacob Astor III, a civilian volunteer. Astor held the honorary rank of colonel and had his own chef, steward and valet.

McClellan's retinue also included royalty: the Comte de Paris, pretender to the throne of France; and his brother, the Duc de

Supplies for General McClellan's Army of the Potomac—artillery, caissons and ammunition—pile up in Washington's Arsenal Park.

Chartres. The two Frenchmen, who had declined any rank above that of honorary captain, were friendly and unassuming, known to their non-French-speaking fellow officers as "Captain Parry and Captain Chatters." Their uncle, the Prince de Joinville, tagged along as an observer and occasionally depicted what he saw in splendid watercolors *(pages 114-123)*.

McClellan had a love of ceremony, and he brought martial pomp to its fullest flower early that autumn in a series of full-dress reviews on the parade ground. At first, the ceremonies consisted of only a few thousand men—one brigade showing off its newly acquired skill at marching and maneuvering. But these were later eclipsed by grand divisional reviews.

Americans had never seen such pageantry. A host of distinguished visitors—senators, Cabinet members, society ladies with hoop skirts and parasols, sometimes even President Lincoln himself—flocked to the parade ground. But the center of attention was always McClellan.

When the blaring of bands on the parade ground stopped, the charismatic general would come galloping down the massed ranks on his great horse. As he swept by, the men under his command would cheer, and McClellan would acknowledge their enthusiasm with a gesture that further endeared him to the troops. "He went beyond the formal military salute," explained one of his officers, "and gave his cap a little twirl, which with his bow and smile seemed to carry a little of personal good fellowship even to the humblest private soldier. If the cheer was repeated he would turn in his saddle and repeat the salute."

The military spectacles elevated the mo-rale of soldier and civilian alike. After one review, a staunch abolitionist named Julia Ward Howe—down from Boston with her physician husband—was riding back to Willard's Hotel in a carriage with several of their friends when the way was blocked by a column of soldiers. Mrs. Howe and her friends, "to beguile the rather tedious drive," began singing popular army songs, including "John Brown's Body." The soldiers cheered the tune, but one of Mrs. Howe's companions suggested that the lyrics could be improved upon.

Back at her hotel, Mrs. Howe awoke before dawn the next day and, inspired by the memory of those marching soldiers, scribbled out new words. Her "Battle Hymn of the Republic," which appeared a few months later in the *Atlantic Monthly*, would soon stir the hearts of Unionists everywhere who regarded the War as a moral crusade against slavery.

McClellan held his climactic parade and review at Bailey's Crossroads, Virginia, approximately seven miles from the Capitol in Washington. "The field," wrote Colonel William Woods Averell of the 3rd Pennsylvania Cavalry, "was a broad amphitheatre, favorable at any part for a view of the whole, and the spectacle of a vast, organized host of 80,000 men in masses of divisions with the artillery and cavalry of each division attached and all its banners floating in the sunlight was the grandest and most inspiring I ever beheld. General McClellan, with his staff, rode rapidly along the fronts of divisions awakening the wildest enthusiasm as he passed. Then the army passed in review and as the ground trembled under the steady tread of the endless columns of disciplined soldiers and the air throbbed with the music

At a barricade on the Washington side of the Chain Bridge, a battery mounts guard against a possible Confederate attack on the capital. The two antiquated Mexican War howitzers trained on the bridge suggest that the chances of invasion by this route were considered slight.

of countless bands, the all pervading feeling was an enthusiastic and ardent admiration for the man who had created the Army of the Potomac. In the realization of all observers, even the most experienced officers, the army was born that day.''

The soldiers' admiration and affection for McClellan was only natural. Largely because of the general and his efforts in their behalf, they were better fed, better trained—better soldiers. "The boys are happy as clams at high water," remarked Private John W.

Chase of the 1st Massachusetts Artillery in a letter to his family. "The rank and file think he is just the man to lead us on to victory when he gets ready and not when Horace Greeley says to go.''

In camp and on the march, the soldiers even celebrated their general in song: "For McClellan's our leader; he is gallant and strong. / For God and our country we are marching along." To a significant degree, the Army of the Potomac had become McClellan's personal army; and that was a mat-

A famous unit revived, Ricketts' Battery of the 1st U.S. Artillery drills in Alexandria. After making a gallant stand, the battery had been shattered at Bull Run, and its

commander, Captain James Ricketts, had been captured. Now reorganized, the outfit would fight its way through the Peninsula under Lieutenant Edmund Kirby.

ter of some concern to earnest republicans who had been raised to fear the ambitions of men on horseback.

One of the few soldiers who did not share in the mass adulation of McClellan was his own immediate superior, General in Chief Winfield Scott. Almost from the moment of McClellan's arrival in Washington, the two men had rubbed each other the wrong way. McClellan was transparently eager for the older man's job—"an ambitious junior," Scott characterized him. And Scott, an infirm giant of a man 75 years old, was surely envious of this trim, vigorous upstart who was young enough to be his grandson. The hero of the Mexican War, and of the War of 1812 before that, suffered from gout, dropsy and vertigo, and he required help in order to rise from his chair.

There were also differences over policy issues. Scott, anxious to keep Regular Army units together to meet emergencies, had stubbornly resisted McClellan's plan to assign capable and energetic young officers of the Regular Army to volunteer units, which needed them badly. "The old General always comes in the way," McClellan wrote his wife. "He understands nothing, appreciates nothing."

Another bone of contention between the old general and the young one was the danger of the Confederate forces in Virginia. McClellan, being a cautious man, continued to overestimate enemy strength, and the tendency was reinforced by faulty intelligence reports. His secret-service chief was Allan Pinkerton, an energetic Scot who had founded one of the first American private-detective agencies.

Pinkerton had done yeoman work for the

Illinois Central when McClellan was an executive there in the late 1850s. After McClellan took command of the Department of Ohio, Pinkerton organized a secret-service bureau for him and then followed the general to Washington. Operating under the *nom de guerre* Major E. J. Allen, Pinkerton later proved to be as adept at catching spies as he was at nabbing bank robbers and railway bandits. For example, he cracked the Washington spy ring headed by Rose Greenhow, who used her considerable feminine wiles to gain access to the plans for the new Washington fortifications and had even hatched a scheme for kidnapping McClellan.

At Camp Pendleton in northern Virginia, a laundress for the 31st Pennsylvania works beside her soldier husband and their children. Army regulations allowed each regiment four washerwomen in camp; in the field, the troops would wash their own clothes.

But Pinkerton's intelligence estimates—based on interrogation of Confederate deserters and prisoners, fugitive slaves and Union sympathizers behind enemy lines—were woefully inaccurate. Early in October, Pinkerton led McClellan to believe that the Confederate forces facing Washington were "not less than 150,000 strong"—well over three times their actual number.

Though Winfield Scott disagreed with McClellan's estimates of enemy strength, he did not argue the point vehemently; he was too much preoccupied by distressing personal differences with McClellan. In despair at the neglect and disrespect McClellan had shown him, he offered to retire, calling himself "an encumbrance to the army as well as to myself." But the President pigeonholed Scott's request, and the old general reluctantly stayed on—to the increasing irritation of his young rival. "Scott," McClellan told his wife, "is the most dangerous antagonist I have."

McClellan was in fact deliberately circumventing his superior officer, dealing directly with the Secretary of War, various Cabinet members and the President. In bypassing proper channels he was abetted by Abraham Lincoln with his strong trust in personal contact. Late of an autumn evening, Lincoln would stroll across from the White House to McClellan's headquarters, located at the northeast corner of Lafayette Square, to discuss strategy.

Face to face in McClellan's first-floor office, the general and his commander in chief made a strange pair: the handsome military man, well-born, dapper, wearing gleaming cavalry boots; and the coarse-featured, towering, ungainly President, the son of a dirt farmer, shabbily dressed and often shod in old leather slippers.

They had gotten to know each other earlier, back in Illinois when Lincoln served as a legal counsel for the Illinois Central Railroad and McClellan was its vice president. McClellan enjoyed listening to Lincoln, with his endless store of anecdotes, but he still did not know quite what to make of Lincoln. "Isn't he a rare bird?" McClellan remarked one night to another officer after a talk with the President.

Lincoln, for his part, was patient with McClellan. He knew his young general was thinking big. Back in August, at the President's request, McClellan had submitted a long memorandum setting forth his strategy for winning the War. The nub of it was McClellan's assertion that the Union could "crush the rebellion at one blow"—if he was given enough troops.

McClellan wanted no fewer than 273,000 men for his Army of the Potomac before he would take the offensive. By early October, however, when he had about half that number on the rolls, some newspapers and politicians had begun to clamor for an advance. The autumn weather was sunny, and the Virginia roads leading south to Richmond were dry and hard. But McClellan remained determined to avoid the kind of premature advance that he felt had brought on the defeat at Bull Run.

"I intend to be careful, and do as well as possible," he told the President on October 10. "Don't let them hurry me, is all I ask."

If Lincoln later recalled his reply, he must have regretted it. For he told McClellan, "You shall have your own way in the matter, I assure you."

Schooling the Army of the Potomac

On July 27, 1861, just six days after Federal forces were routed at Bull Run, their newly appointed commander, George B. McClellan, urged his dispirited troops to find courage in discipline. "Let an honest pride be felt," his order read, "in possessing that high virtue of a soldier, obedience."

Neither obedience nor discipline was commonly cherished by the raw recruits who thronged the camps in the Washington area. Few had any experience of military organization, and many found it distressingly undemocratic that free Americans should be expected to kowtow to a handful of lordly officers. However, those who heeded the lessons of Bull Run accepted one officer's dictum that "without discipline an army is a mob, and the larger the worse." All would have manifold opportunities to practice obedience.

Soldiers of the 1st Connecticut Heavy Artillery march through their camp adjacent to Fort Richardson, Virginia, one link in the chain of strongpoints defending

The schooling of the Army of the Potomac for battle consisted almost entirely of frequent, repetitive drilling—five to eight hours a day. For textbooks, the officers relied on drill manuals that prescribed in minute detail every soldierly act, from loading a rifle to maneuvering in dense regiments a thousand strong. The men in the ranks simply followed orders.

The goal of drill was to move disciplined manpower into position to deliver maximum firepower. This required troops—according to the prevailing military theories of the day—to advance in closely massed formation, and to maneuver and fire in concert. A man had to obey blindly if he was to march forward into a hail of enemy fire. But more than that, he had to follow orders so automatically that even amid the brain-fogging fear and frenzy of battle he would still respond to orders and act as part of a cohesive unit.

Energetic drilling continued for eight full months. But in the end the recruits would have to learn their last lessons from a crueler teacher: experience. "It takes a raw recruit some time to learn that he is not to think or suggest, but obey," wrote a veteran of many battles. "Some never do learn. I acquired it at last, in humility and mud."

Washington. Within the walls of the fort, white-gloved officers stand beside one of the regiment's cannon.

The 2nd Rhode Island Infantry drills by company under the supervision of its officers in a field near Washington. Each company is executing a different movement

including parade rest, guard against cavalry, present arms, right shoulder shift, support arms and shoulder arms.

Bayonets fixed and muskets polished, the 96th Pennsylvania marches off to drill in column of companies, the regimental formation used for the charge into battle. To

keep the men in tight formation, each was required to touch elbows with those flanking him and to march within 13 inches of the man ahead.

Troops of the 17th New York march in review with shouldered muskets and full field packs. Behind the regiment's mounted officers, archways decorated with holiday

evergreen boughs mark the entrance to company streets, lined with conical Sibley tents.

Clash at Ball's Bluff

"At Ball's Bluff, I was hit at 4:30 p.m. I felt as if a horse had kicked me. First Sergeant Smith grabbed me and lugged me to the rear and opened my shirt and ecce! two holes in my breast."

LIEUTENANT OLIVER WENDELL HOLMES JR., 20TH MASSACHUSETTS INFANTRY

2

While the President of the United States was trying to deal with the consequences of defeat at Bull Run, the President of the Confederate States was attempting to cope with some unexpected consequences of victory.

The man eulogized throughout the South as the Hero of Manassas—as the Bull Run battle was known in the Confederacy—was the already-crowned Hero of Sumter, the dashing Louisiana Frenchman, General Pierre Gustave Toutant Beauregard. The fact that the demands on him at Sumter had been slight and his performance at Manassas flawed made little difference; the South no less than the North needed heroes, and Beauregard, charismatic and highly visible, fit the bill. He relished the role and immediately set to work improving on it.

A few days after Bull Run he wrote a letter to two friends in the Confederate Congress. The letter, which they shared with their colleagues, suggested that the government's failure to supply his troops adequately had prevented him from pushing on to capture Washington. The lawmakers were thunderstruck and asked Jefferson Davis to respond.

The President pointed out, in a friendly letter to Beauregard, that there was no evidence that any supply problem had prevented the pursuit of Union forces after the battle. Beauregard quickly backed away from the controversy. But he reminded Davis that friends were urging him to run against Davis in the national election soon to be held—though he assured the President that he would do no such thing. (Davis had been elected in February of 1861 by the convention of seceded states; until reelected by popular vote, he was serving as provisional head of the government.)

Not long afterward, Beauregard submitted his report of the battle. In it he seemed to be claiming full credit for the timely arrival on the field of General Joseph E. Johnston's forces. In a stiffly worded note, Davis challenged Beauregard's assertions and accused him of trying "to exalt yourself at my expense." In fact, Johnston himself deserved the credit for rushing his men from the Shenandoah Valley to Manassas. Beauregard had merely sent a wire appealing for help, and Davis had simply endorsed the appeal and urged Johnston to go to Beauregard's aid.

Beauregard responded to Davis' criticism with a defensive and self-justifying open letter published in a Richmond newspaper under the heading "Within hearing of the Enemy's Guns." Even the general's friends found the letter somewhat tasteless.

While all this correspondence was going on, Beauregard was engaged in an even more bewildering exchange of views with the Confederate War Department. On the battlefield at Manassas, Beauregard had been left in charge of the Confederate forces by his superior, General Johnston, who arrived after the battle had begun and was reluctant to take over without fully understanding the terrain and troop deployments. Beauregard had enjoyed the autonomy, and now he seemed to

A bereaved woman, peering at a portrait of her deceased soldier, graces the sheet-music cover of "The Vacant Chair," a sentimental song inspired by the death of a Federal officer in the Battle of Ball's Bluff in October 1861. Despite its Northern origin, the song was widely published in the South; this edition bears a Richmond imprint.

be trying to perpetuate it; he kept insisting that his corps constituted an independent command. He simply could not seem to understand, said Secretary of War Judah P. Benjamin, that he was second to Johnston "in command of the whole army and not first in command of half the army."

Beauregard finally appealed the matter to the President. At last the exasperated administration gave up on the Hero of Sumter and Manassas and sent him west to serve under Albert Sidney Johnston.

Joseph Johnston, meanwhile, was devoting himself as assiduously as McClellan to "preparing our troops for active service by diligent instruction." As he did so a lull settled over northern Virginia. In the two and a half months following Bull Run there was scarcely any fighting to speak of—only pickets exchanging shots along the upper and lower stretches of the Potomac, and an occasional brief skirmish between patrols.

In fact, late in September Johnston concluded that some of his forward positions were vulnerable to McClellan's growing army, and he began pulling back. On September 27, he evacuated Munson's Hill, his outpost nearest Washington, and fell back to Fairfax Court House, leaving behind so-called Quaker guns—logs emplaced like cannon to deceive the enemy. Then, on October 17, he withdrew from Fairfax Court House and began consolidating his 41,000 men in a triangular area with Centreville at the apex and a base running from Manassas Junction to the Bull Run battlefield.

Word of these Confederate withdrawals came as a pleasant surprise to George McClellan. His men occupied the abandoned positions without firing a shot, considerably deepening the Federal foothold on the Con-

federate side of the Potomac. Then the general noticed an outlying position that the Confederates had not yet abandoned. This was at Leesburg, Virginia, 35 miles up the Potomac from Washington. The Confederates had occupied Leesburg early in August, and it now represented the extreme left flank of their line. McClellan thought that a show of Union force might "shake the enemy out of Leesburg"—without a fight.

That notion would come back to haunt McClellan, for it sparked a chain of events that would lead to a Federal disaster at a place called Ball's Bluff. The fiasco there would reveal that McClellan had not yet remedied all the ills that plagued the Federals at Bull Run. The U.S. Army still suffered from unseasoned officers, failures of communication, a loosely run command structure—faults for which McClellan, as overall commander, would be held accountable.

The misadventure began on October 19, when McClellan sent orders to Brigadier General George A. McCall, whose 13,000-man division was camped on the Virginia side of the Potomac near Langley. McCall's men probed upriver and inland to Dranesville, about 15 miles southeast of Leesburg.

The next morning, McClellan dispatched an order to Brigadier General Charles P. Stone, commander of a division stationed at Poolesville, on the Maryland side of the river roughly eight miles east of Leesburg. He informed Stone that McCall had occupied Dranesville and was sending out a heavy reconnaissance from there, and he told Stone to keep "a good lookout upon Leesburg" to see if McCall's movement would indeed cause the enemy to abandon the town. Then McClellan added a suggestion: "Perhaps a

slight demonstration on your part would have the effect to move them.''

Stone, at 37, was an experienced soldier. Like McClellan, he had graduated high in his class at West Point and served with valor in the Mexican War. As inspector general of the District of Columbia militia, he had succeeded in maintaining order during the hectic April days before troops from the North could rush to Washington's defense.

Stone quickly complied with McClellan's orders. He moved most of his 10,000 men from Poolesville, to the nearby shore of the Potomac. That afternoon, at Edwards Ferry, a few miles southeast of Leesburg, he had his artillery throw a few shells across the river. Then he loaded up three boats with 35 men each, sent them over to the Virginia shore and, a short while later, brought them back. This was the "slight demonstration" McClellan had suggested—a small show of force that might persuade the Confederates at Leesburg that a major attack was in the offing.

Then Stone dutifully sent out a patrol to maintain "a good lookout upon Leesburg." The patrol consisted of 20 men under Captain Charles Philbrick of the 15th Massachusetts Infantry, which had taken up positions on Harrison's Island, about three miles upstream from Edwards Ferry. This narrow island, three miles long, divided the Potomac into two branches.

Philbrick's patrol left the island in small boats that evening of October 20 and paddled the 60 yards to the Virginia shore. There they landed at the foot of a steep bank known to the locals as Ball's Bluff. Nearly 100 feet high, studded with rocks and covered with tangles of mountain laurel, the bluff was named after former owners of the land, the family of George Wash-

In one of many artillery exchanges across the Potomac, Federal batteries in Maryland shell Confederate forces stationed on the Virginia side in October 1861. Mounted officers, at left, observe the barrage through field glasses.

ington's mother, Mary Ball Washington.

Philbrick followed an old cow path up the bluff. It grew dark as he led his men through the woods toward Leesburg, and they picked their way carefully in the hazy moonlight. Three quarters of a mile along the route inland, Philbrick saw something on a ridge up ahead. It appeared to be a Confederate encampment of about 30 tents, with no guards in sight.

The Federals quickly retraced their steps. They reached Harrison's Island at about 10 p.m., and Philbrick dispatched news of the unguarded enemy camp to General Stone, who was still downstream at Edwards Ferry.

Stone, having thus far carried out McClellan's vague orders to the letter, took a fateful step beyond. Philbrick's report of an unguarded camp suggested to him that the Confederates might be pulling out of Leesburg. Stone launched a double reconnais-

sance in force. He personally supervised one crossing at Edwards Ferry; several companies boated to the opposite shore without incident. At the same time, he sent Colonel Charles Devens, commander of the 15th Massachusetts, to lead the second, more aggressive crossing at Ball's Bluff.

Devens, a 41-year-old militia officer and noted Boston lawyer, shoved off from Harrison's Island at about midnight. His force, five companies numbering 300 men, had only three small boats, capable of carrying 10 men each, so the crossing took nearly four hours. His orders were to attack and destroy the Confederate camp reported by Captain Philbrick, then return to Harrison's Island unless he could find a beachhead that could be held with the help of reinforcements.

Before dawn, Devens was joined at the top of the bluff by 100 additional men, sent across the river under Colonel William R.

Lee to cover the withdrawal. Lee, a doughty old West Pointer, commanded the 20th Massachusetts Infantry, which was known as the Harvard Regiment because so many of its officers had attended that institution. Lee's detachment was to remain at the top of the bluff to cover Devens' return.

About daybreak on October 21, Devens and his men set out toward Leesburg to look for the unguarded Confederate camp. They found the right ridge, but it soon became clear that the camp did not exist, and never had. The tents had been an illusion caused by hazy moonlight filtering through a row of trees.

But Devens moved on. From a ridge not much more than a mile from Leesburg, he could look down into the town. He saw four tents but no other sign of the enemy. Devens sent back a messenger to tell Stone he could hold on in front of Ball's Bluff until reinforced.

Though Devens could not see them, there were plenty of Confederates around. An entire Confederate brigade of 2,000 men was encamped along the Leesburg Turnpike several miles southeast of the town. The Confederate commander, Colonel Nathan G. Evans, had moved there early the previous day to meet the threat posed when the Federals under General McCall occupied Dranesville to the southeast. Evans had his pickets out in all directions. During the night, a detachment of Confederates had been on sentinel duty less than a mile upriver from Ball's Bluff, and they had detected the sounds of Devens' predawn crossing.

Now the Confederate detachment, numbering about 40 men, was heading back toward Leesburg to avoid being cut off by an apparent Federal thrust from Ball's Bluff. At about 7 a.m. they stumbled onto Devens' Federals. There, in a field where corn was standing in shocks, a sharp skirmish ensued. This clash was the opening round in the Battle of Ball's Bluff.

Both sides sent in reinforcements. Colonel Evans now knew that two groups of Federals had crossed the river three miles apart—at Ball's Bluff and at Edwards Ferry. He sent three of his four regiments to block the road leading to Leesburg from the crossing at Edwards Ferry. And to hold Devens in check in front of Ball's Bluff, he sent seven companies of infantry and cavalry—about 400 men— to join the 40 Confederates who had happened upon Devens' force.

Under this new pressure, Devens fell back toward the bluff. There he was joined by the remaining five companies of his regiment—and five more companies of the 20th Massachusetts—668 men who had crossed over from Harrison's Island in the course of the morning. Thus reinforced, Devens moved forward again, and the skirmishing continued inconclusively.

Around noon, however, the Confederate commander began to gain control. Nathan Evans, an experienced officer and Indian fighter who had held gallantly against the opening Federal attack in the battle at Bull Run, was now at his namesake, Fort Evans, a cluster of rough earthworks a little over a mile south of the fighting. Evans was 37 years old, with a black beard, piercing eyes and a reputation as a hard drinker. An artilleryman who saw him at Fort Evans that day said he sat on horseback "imbibing generously. When inspiration was slow in coming from Above, he invoked the aid of his canteen hanging at his side."

A tough fighting man, Colonel Nathan G. Evans was promoted to brigadier general for his skillful handling of the Confederate forces at Ball's Bluff. Stubborn independence and his fondness for drink led to two courts-martial in 1863. Though acquitted both times, Evans was eventually relieved of command.

For all his tippling, Evans was a keen tactician. Sensing that the main action around Leesburg would occur at Ball's Bluff, he began hurrying regiments in that direction. The first of these regiments to join the attack was Colonel Eppa Hunton's 8th Virginia—described by a Confederate officer as "375 more people in bad temper." As the 8th attacked, Devens' troops fell back 60 paces. Then, at about 2:15 p.m., the Federals retreated all the way to a large open field fronting Ball's Bluff.

Atop the bluff, Devens found a stream of new reinforcements struggling up the cow path. Their commander was Colonel Edward D. Baker, a tall, handsome, clean-shaven man, with a ruddy face and a high forehead fringed with gray hair. Baker welcomed Devens exuberantly: "I congratulate you, sir, upon the prospect of a battle."

Baker, 50 years old, was no ordinary colonel. He was a U.S. Senator from Oregon and a longtime confidant of Abraham Lincoln. The two men had become close friends while they were young lawyers in Illinois. Baker was once threatened at a rowdy political meeting there, and Lincoln had vowed to break a stone water jug over the head of anyone who laid a hand on his colleague. They had stayed in touch after Baker went west to California and later Oregon, and Lincoln named his second son after his old friend.

After the firing on Fort Sumter, Baker had raised a regiment that was composed predominantly of Philadelphians but was known as the 1st California Regiment in honor of Baker's days in that state. Though he rose to command of a brigade, Baker refused Lincoln's attempt to promote him to brigadier general, saying such rank would be incompatible with his role as a senator. Baker kept his seat in the Senate, rushing in from camp in full uniform, unbuckling his sword and rising to lend his booming voice to debates over the War.

On the day before the Battle of Ball's Bluff, Baker had stopped at the White House and stretched out on the lawn to chat with the President. As he left to join his brigade across the Potomac from Leesburg, Mrs. Lincoln handed Baker a bouquet of late autumn flowers. "Very beautiful," said Baker. Then he added a strange, unforgettable remark: "These flowers and my memory will wither together."

Soldiers naturally tend to think of death before going into battle, and Baker had good cause; he was as green as most young volunteers in spite of his promising success as a military administrator. His time under fire

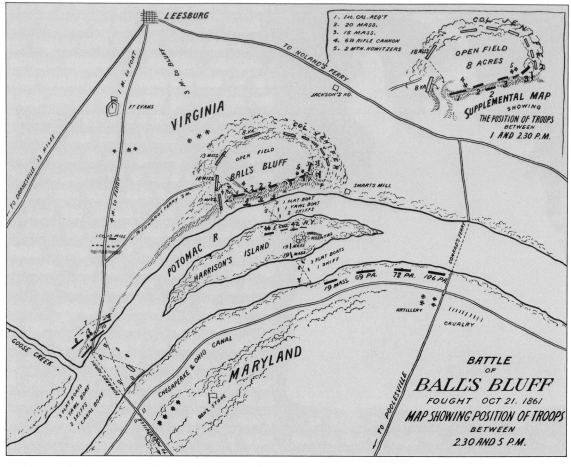

1. 1st. CAL. REG'T
2. 20 MASS.
3. 15 MASS.
4. 6th RIFLE CANNON
5. 2 MTN. HOWITZERS

SUPPLEMENTAL MAP
SHOWING
THE POSITION OF TROOPS
BETWEEN
1 AND 2.30 P.M.

BATTLE
OF
BALL'S BLUFF
FOUGHT OCT 21. 1861
MAP SHOWING POSITION OF TROOPS
BETWEEN
2.30 AND 5 P.M.

This period map shows the upper Potomac around Ball's Bluff, where Federal and Confederate forces clashed on October 21, 1861. A Federal brigade crossed the river at Harrison's Island and climbed the bluff; there the troops were routed in a stiff fight by Confederate reinforcements brought up from Leesburg. The Federals might have been helped by a second force at Edwards Ferry, but it withdrew.

had been limited to undistinguished service as commander of a volunteer regiment during the Mexican War. Nonetheless, General Stone had given Baker wide discretion in deploying his brigade. Baker could either reinforce the regiments of Devens and Lee or order them back to Harrison's Island.

Being a romantic, Baker had quickly made a romantic decision. Without bothering to find out what was happening on the bluff, he sent two of his regiments across the river, the 1st California and the predominantly Irish 42nd New York Infantry, known as the Tammany Regiment. Baker then wasted more than an hour helping to bring a large flatboat from the nearby Chesapeake and Ohio

Canal to the Maryland shore to facilitate the crossing to Harrison's Island—work better left to a subordinate. For all practical purposes, he did nothing to organize a more efficient ferry system between the island and the bluff, which was being served by only a handful of boats.

After Baker reached the bluff and greeted Devens, he began deploying his troops in the open field. The field was about 10 acres in extent and roughly trapezoidal in shape—perhaps 800 feet deep and 600 feet wide at its broadest point, which was at the end away from the river. Baker deployed his battle line across the near third of the field, parallel to the river, with each wing extending into the woods on either side. On the right, in the woods, his line formed a dogleg with the flank thrust forward.

It was not a good formation. To the left front of the field, beyond a ravine, rose a cluster of wooded hills that commanded the Federal position. Besides failing to seize the heights, Baker had aligned his right flank in such a way that the companies there would be unable to fire to the front if the center of the line advanced. In addition, Baker had placed his reserves behind the battle line in a position fully exposed to Confederate snipers.

Those snipers, hidden in the woods that

surrounded the field on three sides, soon began to take a toll. But Baker seemed unconcerned. When he saw Colonel Milton Cogswell, commander of the Tammany Regiment, coming up the cow path from the river at about 2:30 p.m., he gaily called out lines from Sir Walter Scott's poem "The Lady of the Lake": "One blast upon your bugle horn is worth a thousand men."

Cogswell, a West Pointer and one of the few professional soldiers on the Federal side that day, ignored the poetry and instantly spotted the worst defect in Baker's troop deployment. He suggested an immediate advance to occupy the high ground to the

Troops of the 15th Massachusetts Infantry launch a bayonet charge on the open field atop Ball's Bluff. This regiment suffered the heaviest losses of any Federal unit that day—302 officers and enlisted men killed, wounded or missing in action.

left. But Baker ignored Cogswell's advice.

It was a bad mistake. Baker's wily opposite number, Colonel Evans, was sending reinforcements. The 18th Mississippi marched up and occupied the precious high ground facing the Federal left. Now the Confederates were only about one regiment shy of equaling the Federal strength of 1,700 men.

At about 3 p.m. the reinforced Confederates increased their fire from the woods, aiming low to compensate for their muskets' trajectory. "The first volley came and the balls flew like hail," wrote Captain William Francis Bartlett of the 20th Massachusetts, whose men lay prone in the right center of the line. "They fired beautifully too, their balls all coming low, within from one to four feet from the ground."

The fire was so intense that the Federals concluded that they were outnumbered by 3 or 4 to 1. (The Confederates, for their part, thought *they* were outnumbered by at least the same margin.) Then, at about 4 p.m., the 17th Mississippi arrived and slipped into the crescent-shaped Confederate line. After that, the opposing forces were roughly equal in strength. In experience, however, the Confederates had a distinct edge: Most of them had been blooded at Bull Run, while nearly all of the Northerners were new to battle.

Despite the heavy Confederate musket fire, the Federals possessed superior firepower for a time. Baker had managed to bring across the river three pieces of artillery—two light mountain howitzers and a rifled James cannon that fired a 12-pound projectile. However, the time required to ferry the guns, ammunition and horses had delayed the crossing of badly needed infantry. And because the cow path up the bluff

was too steep for the horses to pull the big James gun, its crew had to take the piece apart, haul it to the top, then reassemble it.

At first, the three guns proved effective. Their shells crashed into the woods, sending splinters from trees into hidden clusters of Confederates. But Baker, in another tactical error, had stationed the artillery in front of his battle line without sufficient infantry support. One by one, the gun crews were picked off by Confederate musket fire. Baker and three other officers tried to take over the guns, but they were inexperienced and ineffectual. After firing no more than eight rounds, the James gun fell silent.

The two howitzers were nearly captured at about 4 p.m. when the 18th Mississippi surged forward. The charge was repulsed, however, and cost the regiment its commander, Colonel Erasmus R. Burt, who was shot from his horse and mortally wounded. During this same charge, a Federal lieutenant just out of Harvard, Oliver Wendell Holmes Jr. of the 20th Massachusetts, was hit by two musket balls. The future justice of the U.S. Supreme Court was carried from the field unconscious and joined the stream of Federal wounded being ferried back to Harrison's Island.

On the Federal left, the commander of the 1st California Regiment, Lieutenant Colonel Isaac Wistar, received his third wound, a shattered right elbow. The first man to reach his side was Colonel Baker, his old law partner in San Francisco and the man who had recruited him for the regiment.

Baker ordered a soldier to get his friend to a boat, then strode back in front of his battle line seemingly "indifferent to bullets," according to a witness. A few minutes later, at about 4:30 p.m., the Federal commander

Amid fierce fighting atop Ball's Bluff, Federal troops carry off their mortally wounded commander, Colonel Edward D. Baker. Confederate soldiers attempting to capture Baker are warded off by his sword-wielding adjutant, Captain Frederick Harvey.

was about 10 paces out in the no man's land between the lines urging on his men when a tall, red-haired Confederate soldier jumped out of the woods and emptied his revolver into him. As Baker crumpled to the ground, there was a mad scramble for his body. Federal soldiers had to struggle hand-to-hand against a Rebel charge before they recovered the body and sent it back across the river.

The plight of the beleaguered Federal force was now desperate. Confederates were pressing in from three sides, squeezing the

Federals back toward the steep bluff. The other Federal colonels wanted to withdraw to the river, but the ranking officer, Colonel Cogswell of the Tammany Regiment, saw one last chance to break out. He thought it might still be possible to cut through on the left and follow the river downstream three miles to hook up with the Federal beachhead opposite Edwards Ferry. Cogswell ordered a column of attack to form on the left. The 15th Massachusetts was brought across from the right to support two recently arrived companies of Cogswell's regiment.

As these dispositions were being made, there occurred a freakish—and decisive—incident. Out of the woods rode a man on a gray horse. He raced in front of the Federal attack column on the left, waved his hat and shouted, "Come on, boys!" The two Tammany companies responded with a yell and surged forward, pulling some of the 15th Massachusetts troops with them. In the excitement and confusion, they had thought the man was one of their own officers. But he was a Confederate, a brigade staff officer, Lieutenant Charles B. Wildman, who had dashed onto the field and had momentarily mistaken the Federals for his own men.

Federal officers managed to halt the soldiers from the 15th Massachusetts after a few steps forward, but the Tammany companies moved ahead into a burst of Confederate fire and were badly cut up. Lieutenant Wildman rode away unharmed.

This strange quirk of battle ended any hope for a breakout on the left. Cogswell ordered his troops to withdraw to the edge of the bluff and prepare for evacuation.

The terrible irony of their plight was that help was agonizingly near. Just several hundred yards away on Harrison's Island, waiting for boats that were slowed by the unloading of the casualties from the battlefield, were perhaps 1,000 Federal soldiers. Nearly twice that many men, also lacking adequate ferry service, waited on the Maryland shore, another few hundred yards to the east.

And three miles downstream from Ball's Bluff, of course, was the Federal beachhead on the Virginia shore opposite Edwards Ferry. General Stone, supervising this operation from the Maryland shore, now had 2,250 men across the river. Until he got word of

Colonel Baker's death shortly after 5 p.m., Stone thought things were going well at Ball's Bluff—Baker had failed to inform him otherwise. Even now, Stone might have gone to the relief of the men at Ball's Bluff.

Three things stopped him. One was the 13th Mississippi, which Evans had left on the road to Edwards Ferry as a blocking force. The unit consisted of no more than 500 men, but it had appeared stronger.

The second thing was a strong Confederate position reported between Edwards Ferry and Ball's Bluff. Stone in his post-battle report referred to this position as "breastworks and a masked battery, which barred the movement of troops from left to right." The existence of this masked battery was never firmly established, though it is possible that Stone was referring to six field guns of the Richmond Howitzers, which Evans was keeping in reserve near his headquarters at Fort Evans.

Finally, at about the time he learned of Baker's death, Stone was also getting wildly exaggerated reports about Confederate strength around Leesburg. When he heard that there might be as many as 10,000 Confederates across the river, he began withdrawing his force opposite Edwards Ferry. Then he rode upstream to take personal command of the forces on Harrison's Island and the Maryland shore opposite it.

There, at about 6 p.m., Stone suddenly remembered McCall's division down at Dranesville. It had been McCall's occupation of Dranesville two days before—and McClellan's subsequent order to Stone for "a slight demonstration"—that had led to the Battle of Ball's Bluff in the first place.

Stone wired McClellan's headquarters in Washington, asking for help from McCall's

Routed Federal troops scramble
down the slope of Ball's Bluff and
plunge into the Potomac. "The river
was covered with a mass of struggling
beings," wrote a Confederate soldier,
"and we kept up a steady fire
upon them as long as the faintest
ripple could be seen."

division. The request took McClellan by surprise. He too had thought the battle at Ball's Bluff was going well; earlier in the day he had even wired Stone, urging him to take Leesburg. (Ironically, the message was in cipher, and Stone did not have the key to decode it.)

As it happened, McCall's division—essential to McClellan's original reconnaissance ploy—no longer occupied Dranesville. Under orders from McClellan to retire when he had completed his reconnaissance work around Dranesville, McCall had finished the job and started the march back to camp at about 8:30 that morning; he was now more than 20 miles from Leesburg. McClellan, in one of the many failures of communication that afflicted the Army of the Potomac that day, had neglected to inform Stone of this crucial fact.

At Ball's Bluff, meanwhile, the final act in this tragic Federal drama was being played out. By 6 p.m. Cogswell's men had fallen back under his orders to the woods fringing the bluff; they stood with their backs to the river, at the edge of the precipice.

Arrayed 100 yards in front of them, silhouetted by the last rays of light, were the Confederates, deployed in conventional battle formation two ranks deep with skirmishers out ahead of them. Bayonets fixed, they were ready for the final advance.

"Charge, Mississippians, charge!" shouted Colonel Winfield Scott Featherston of the 17th Mississippi. "Drive them into the Potomac or into eternity!"

The Confederates rose from a kneeling position and moved forward across the open field. When they were about 50 yards from the foe they began firing. Clinton Hatcher, the giant color-bearer for the 8th Virginia, was shot dead within a few feet of the Federal line. The Confederates kept advancing and firing until their gray coats mixed with Federal blue and the bayonet replaced bullet.

Many of the Federals managed to flee down to the river on the cow path under heavy Confederate fire. But others were driven to the brink of the bluff, where they faced an even more perilous descent. The scene here was described by a young Confederate soldier, Randolph Abbot Shotwell:

"A kind of shiver ran through the huddled mass upon the brow of the cliff; it gave way, rushed a few steps; then, in one wild panic-stricken herd, rolled, leaped, tumbled over the precipice. Screams of pain and terror filled the air. Men seemed suddenly bereft of reason, they leaped over the bluff with muskets still in their clutch, threw themselves into the river without divesting themselves of their heavy accoutrements, hence went to the bottom like lead. Others sprang down upon the heads and bayonets of those below. A gray-haired private of the 1st California was found with his head mashed between two rocks by the heavy boots of a ponderous 'Tammany' man, who had broken his own neck by the fall! The side of the bluff was worn smooth by the number sliding down."

Below, on the narrow beach between bluff and river, the scene was no less chaotic. Federal soldiers scrambled through the gathering dusk in a futile search for boats. Two of the small boats had disappeared, and a metal skiff was so riddled with bullets that it soon sank. A large flatboat laden with 30 or more of the wounded capsized when able-bodied fugitives from the bluff jumped aboard; the wounded flailed helplessly in the 18-foot-deep waters of the rain-swollen Potomac.

But many Federal officers showed remarkable poise amid the chaos. Captains

Captain Alois Babo (*seated*) and Lieutenant Reinhold Wesselhoeft, commanding a company of German immigrants in the 20th Massachusetts Infantry, were among the more than 100 men drowned or shot at Ball's Bluff as they tried to swim across the Potomac after the Federal defeat.

The body of a Federal soldier who died at Ball's Bluff is pulled from the Potomac 19 miles downstream at Great Falls on the Maryland shore

William Bartlett of the 20th Massachusetts and Timothy O'Meara of the Tammany Regiment took some of their men up the bluff for one last skirmish. Then Bartlett led a group of about 80 along the shore to Smart's Mill, three quarters of a mile upstream, where the water was less turbulent. He recovered a skiff from the shallow bottom and, calmly brandishing his pistol to enforce order, succeeded in sending the entire group across, five men at a time, to safety on the northern tip of Harrison's Island. O'Meara, meanwhile, remained as a rear guard at the bluff until overwhelmed and captured.

Colonel Devens of the 15th Massachusetts ordered his men to discard their weapons and swim for it. Devens was then sent safely across on a log by a group of his men. Two companies of the 15th were carrying new rifled muskets, and these men refused to part with their prized weapons. They strapped them on their backs and dived in. Some of these men reached Harrison's Island.

From atop the bluff, Confederate soldiers watched the river overwhelm the screaming, dying men. The Confederates kept on firing until—one of them recalled—"darkness shut in the bloody work and night in mercy drew her sable curtain over the dead."

Exactly 529 Federal prisoners were round-

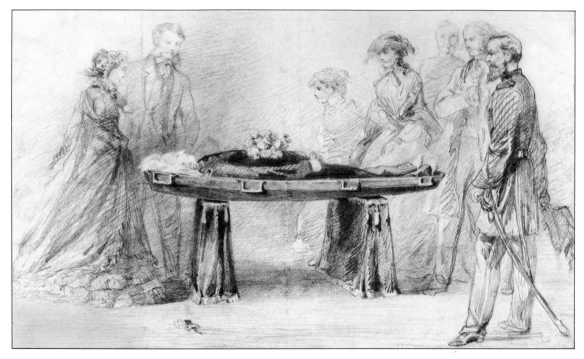

Colonel Edward Baker's body lies in state in a Washington funeral home before being sent west for burial in Baker's adopted state of California. President Lincoln, along with many other officials, later attended a memorial service for his longtime friend on December 11, 1861.

ed up, including Colonels Cogswell and Lee and Major Paul Joseph Revere of the 20th Massachusetts, grandson of the Revolutionary War patriot. All were marched off to prison in Richmond. In Washington, the Federal command reported that 49 men were found dead on the field and 198 wounded. More than 100 others were probably drowned. In sharp contrast to these losses, which amounted to more than 50 per cent of the 1,700 Federals who saw action at Ball's Bluff, the Confederates reported only 36 killed, 117 wounded and two missing.

The Federal losses were small compared with the battle casualties suffered at Bull Run. But they were appalling for a little fight of no strategic significance. All in all, the sharp reverse at Ball's Bluff, coming in the midst of McClellan's much heralded rebuilding of the Army of the Potomac, stunned the North. *Harper's Weekly* said, "History affords few examples of such slaughter,"

and *Leslie's Illustrated* concluded somberly: "This time military incompetence must accept its own responsibilities. The battle was not a great military blunder, but a great military crime."

President Lincoln was shocked and anguished by the defeat and the loss of his friend. He was sitting in McClellan's headquarters when the telegraph clicked the news of Baker's death, and tears came to his eyes. McClellan tried to comfort him. "There is many a good fellow that wears the shoulderstraps going under the sod before this thing is over," he said. "There is no loss too great to be repaired. If I should get knocked on the head, Mr. President, you will put another man immediately into my shoes."

Lincoln knew he needed McClellan. He looked at his young general and said, "I want you to take care of yourself."

For his part, McClellan was saddened by Ball's Bluff. He was also embarrassed, for in one of his proclamations to the troops before the battle, he had declared grandly, "Soldiers! We have seen our last retreat. We have seen our last defeat." Still, the looseness of command that led to defeat was a fault McClellan shared with General Stone, who would eventually bear the heaviest onus of blame. And generals could not afford to be thin-skinned over a minor defeat; McClellan's defense of his conduct proved that he was quite adept at taking care of himself.

Four days after Ball's Bluff, on the night of October 25, McClellan met for three hours with a group of angry senators. They were searching for a scapegoat, and they demanded an advance by McClellan's army to atone for the defeat.

A new offensive was the last thing McClellan wanted. Indeed, Ball's Bluff with its tactical and command blunders and looseness of command only reinforced his conviction that the Army of the Potomac was not yet ready for action. That night, McClellan coolly disclaimed responsibility for the defeat and managed to divert the wrath of the senators by arguing that General in Chief Winfield Scott was the real problem. He implied that the old general was an impediment to active operations and made the proper coordination of forces impossible.

The senators were convinced. They put pressure on Lincoln, and less than a week later the President accepted Scott's offer of retirement, which first had been tendered back in August. Scott proposed as his successor Major General Henry W. Halleck, a brilliant military theoretician who commanded the Federal Department of Missouri. But Lincoln turned instead to the young organizational genius who had created the Army of

the Potomac. On the 1st of November, he designated McClellan general in chief of all Federal armies.

This post was an enormous responsibility. The Union now had more than half a million soldiers spread out from coast to coast. Lincoln worried about whether McClellan could shoulder the new load while retaining personal command of the Army of the Potomac. McClellan had no doubts. "I can do it all," he told the President.

Two days later, on the morning of November 3, McClellan arose at 4 a.m. and, with his staff and a squadron of cavalry, rode through the darkness and pouring rain to see General Scott off at the train station. This was the old wooden depot near the Capitol where McClellan had arrived from western Virginia to take command of a routed and demoralized army. In just three months he had hammered that defeated rabble into a well-trained force of 168,000 men, and had become the commanding officer of the entire U.S. Army.

In the station the two generals exchanged pleasantries. General Scott sent special regards to Mrs. McClellan and her new baby. Then the old warrior was helped aboard the train for New York; he planned to visit his daughter before proceeding to France for medical attention.

The scene in the dimly lit depot lingered in McClellan's mind. Later that day he wrote his wife: "I saw there the end of a long, active, and ambitious life, the end of the career of the first soldier of his nation; and it was a feeble old man scarce able to walk; hardly any one there to see him off but his successor. Should I ever become vainglorious and ambitious, remind me of that spectacle."

Music for Making War

Music was as much a part of army life during the War as hardtack and coffee. Regimental brass bands kept time for the troops as they marched off to war, and thereafter their activities in camp and on the battlefield were regulated by bugle calls or the roll of drums. Small wonder that General Robert E. Lee declared, "I don't believe we can have an army without music."

During the first two years of the War more than 28,000 men joined Federal and Confederate bands, including thousands of professional musicians whose services were recruited—and even paid for—by the officers of local militia regiments. While the great majority of the musicians joined regimental bands, each of the 10 companies in a regiment also had its own musicians who transmitted orders with drum and fife or with bugle calls. The companies' musicians occasionally were grouped together to form an impromptu band or drum corps. This practice became commonplace in the Federal armies after July 1862, when Congress cut back the number of bands to no more than one for every brigade.

The bands served primarily as morale builders: They welcomed recruits, entertained in camp, inspired troops on the march or in battle, and celebrated victories. But the bandsmen also served in a dangerous role. During battles, they often laid down their instruments, reported to the regimental surgeon and went out to rescue the wounded from the battlefield.

Resplendent in brass-buttoned blue frock coats emblazoned with regimental numerals, the band of the 4th Vermont Volunteers assembles for a group portrait. The bandsmen followed their fighting comrades all through the Peninsular Campaign.

The Mellow Brass of a Marching Band

On their first furlough of the War, in
July 1862, bandsmen of the 26th
North Carolina Infantry Regiment
(*above*) show off their instruments
and uniforms. The horns they carried
ranged in pitch from the mellow E-flat
Flügelhorn (*top left*) down to the deep
bass saxhorn tuba (*lower left*), whose
backward-thrust bell directed the
music to troops following the band.

Calls of Drum and Fife

The instruments used by fifers and drummers were simple and effective. The drums, carried on shoulder straps, were often blazoned with colorful insignia, such as the Federal eagle at right, or with decorative designs like the floral pattern above on an instrument used by a North Carolina drummer.

Each infantry company traditionally had one drummer and one fifer. These musicians—often boys considered too young to fight—played the dozen or so distinctive calls that summoned troops in camp to meals, drills, chores and inspections. In the field, they drummed and piped the calls that announced major movements or battle orders. The most frequently heard call in the field was the so-called general, which signaled the men to strike tents and prepare to move out. The roll was begun by the headquarters drummers and then picked up by the drummers of every company, until the beat reached a rumbling crescendo that one observer called "at once magnificent and horrifying."

CONFEDERATE DRUMMER'S COAT

Bugles for Cavalry and Artillery

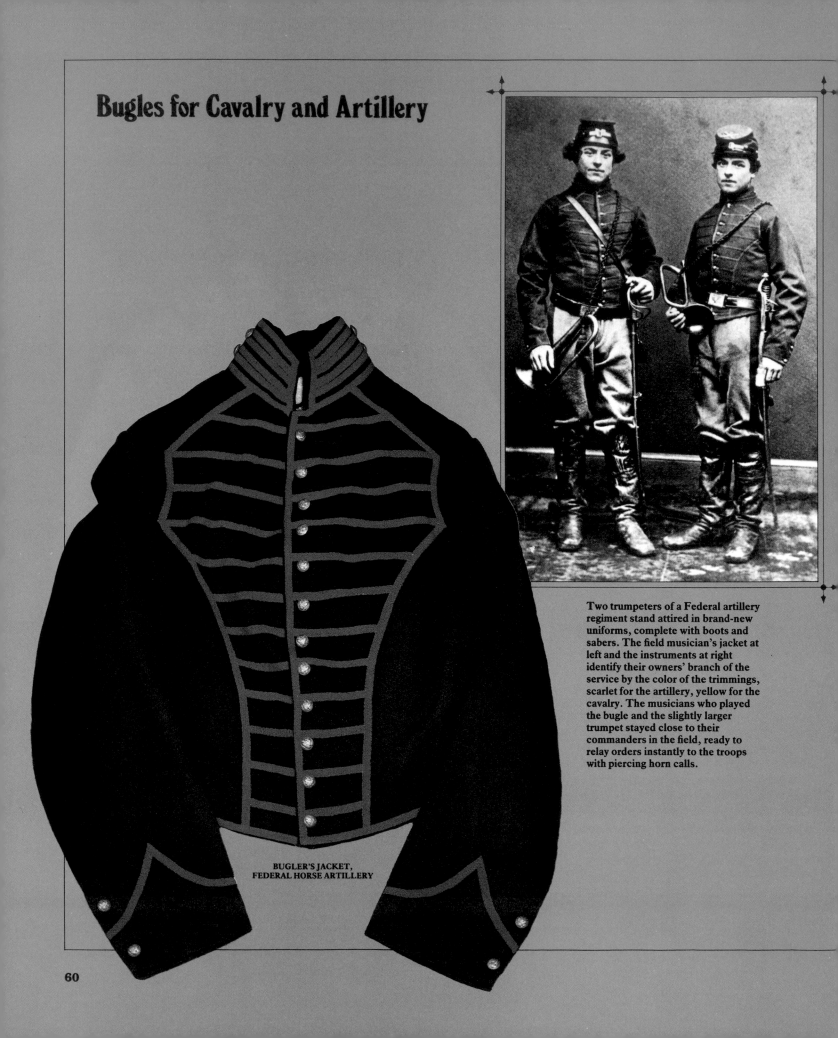

**BUGLER'S JACKET,
FEDERAL HORSE ARTILLERY**

Two trumpeters of a Federal artillery regiment stand attired in brand-new uniforms, complete with boots and sabers. The field musician's jacket at left and the instruments at right identify their owners' branch of the service by the color of the trimmings, scarlet for the artillery, yellow for the cavalry. The musicians who played the bugle and the slightly larger trumpet stayed close to their commanders in the field, ready to relay orders instantly to the troops with piercing horn calls.

CONFEDERATE CAVALRY BUGLE

FEDERAL CAVALRY TRUMPET

The Troublesome Commanders

On the evening of November 13, 1861, less than two weeks after he had named George McClellan general in chief of all the Union armies, Abraham Lincoln strolled over to his young general's home and headquarters, only a block from the White House, to discuss strategy.

Lincoln did not claim to have any knowledge of military matters, but as President of a nation at war he was doing his best to learn whatever he could. He took a special interest in new weapons, encouraging inventors and personally trying out rifles in a weed-grown lot known as Treasury Park, south of the White House. To bone up on strategy and tactics, he borrowed military treatises from the Library of Congress and chatted often with his commanders. He had conferred almost daily with General Scott and now he met frequently with McClellan, who was a keen student of military science.

On this particular night, however, Lincoln was to learn a different kind of lesson. The attitude of the young general toward the President was changing rapidly. At the door of McClellan's house, Lincoln was informed by a servant that the general was not at home, but was expected soon. Lincoln and his two companions—Secretary of State William H. Seward and John Hay, one of the President's private secretaries—took seats in the parlor and waited.

After about an hour, McClellan arrived.

Ignoring a servant's announcement of his distinguished visitors, the general proceeded upstairs, passing the door of the parlor without a word of greeting. Lincoln waited 30 minutes more, then asked a servant to tell McClellan he had guests. The answer came back that the general had gone to bed.

In his usual self-effacing manner, Lincoln shrugged off the obvious snub. When John Hay expressed anger at this unparalleled "insolence of epaulettes," the President said it was no time to be worrying about etiquette and personal dignity.

Hay quite rightly saw the general's behavior that night as "a portent." It was one of the first public indications of McClellan's growing alienation from civilian political authority. By then the general was already leveling invective at offending officials in daily letters to his wife. Politicians were "wretched" or "these incapables." The Cabinet contained "some of the greatest geese I have ever seen." As for Lincoln, he was "the original Gorilla."

The immediate cause of McClellan's irritation was the rising public clamor for action. Once again, Horace Greeley's New York *Tribune* was trumpeting the old battle cry that had been silenced by the disaster at Bull Run—"Forward to Richmond!" Even if the Army of the Potomac was not yet ready to mount an offensive against the Confederate capital, there were those who felt that McClellan should at least at-

A youthful private of the 18th Massachusetts stands with crossed arms in a French chasseur uniform, one of 10,000 bought by the U.S. government in 1861 to help clothe the Army. General George McClellan awarded the jaunty outfits to regiments that displayed special proficiency in drill.

tempt operations against lesser objectives.

The likeliest targets were two Confederate outposts that were interrupting the flow of supplies into Washington. One was a stretch of railroad above Harpers Ferry, 50 miles northwest of the city; here Confederate raiders had recently ripped up 25 miles of track along the Baltimore & Ohio line, breaking Washington's rail link to the West. The other sore spot was about 25 miles south of Washington, on the Virginia side of the lower Potomac, where the Confederates had installed batteries of artillery that effectively blockaded merchant shipping headed for the capital.

McClellan considered these Confederate outposts mere thorns that would be removed when he mounted his major thrust south. Earlier in the fall, McClellan had intended to direct that thrust against the main body of Confederates entrenched around Centreville and Manassas—and he had planned to do so no later than Thanksgiving. But for a number of reasons McClellan's thinking changed during November.

He began developing a novel plan that would make it possible for his army to bypass the Centreville-Manassas stronghold entirely. He would load his troops aboard ships and steam from Annapolis through Chesapeake Bay to the mouth of the Rappahannock River. A few miles up the Rappahannock they would land at Urbanna, a tiny hamlet about 60 road miles northeast of Richmond. His army would then march on the Confederate capital.

McClellan's Urbanna plan had a number of attractive features. It would cut more than 50 miles off the marching distance to Richmond, and he could traverse that distance without having to fight a battle.

The Confederate forces would be outflanked and compelled to evacuate their Centreville-Manassas stronghold, and they would have to rush south to defend their capital without adequate preparation. With luck, McClellan's columns might even reach Richmond before the Confederates from northern Virginia. Finally, and perhaps best of all from McClellan's point of view, the Urbanna plan would give him added weeks to train the Army of the Potomac, for it would take that long to assemble the great fleet of ships needed to transport the 100,000 soldiers designated for this assault, together with all their baggage.

McClellan discussed the Urbanna plan with several influential men, including Secretary of the Treasury Salmon P. Chase. But neither McClellan nor anyone else breathed a word of it to the President. The general had avoided Lincoln since leaving him waiting on the evening of November 13. McClellan's attitude toward the President was colored by his developing disdain for Republican politicians, "a set of men unscrupulous and false." McClellan was a Democrat, and he felt sure that the Republicans held that against him—as indeed they did. Above all, he was a soldier in the tradition of Napoleon, and he bitterly resented political interference in his plans. He was convinced that he alone could save the Union, provided only he was left alone by " 'browsing' Presidents."

Lincoln learned nothing about the Urbanna plan through November and into early December. Then, for lack of any plan from McClellan, he sent the general in chief his own proposal for a frontal and flank attack against the Confederates at Centreville-Manassas. McClellan sat on the President's plan for more than a week. Finally, on the 10th of December, he turned aside Lincoln's suggested offensive. He had recently received information, he wrote, indicating that "the enemy would meet us in front with equal forces nearly." Instead, "I have now my mind actually turned towards another plan of campaign that I do not think at all anticipated by the enemy, nor by many of our own people."

Beyond this enigmatic reference, McClellan told the President nothing of his plan. But Lincoln had only to look about the city to see that, whatever McClellan had in mind, it would not happen soon. The first snow had fallen, and the soldiers of the Army of the Potomac—now nearly 200,000 strong—were busy building log huts to serve as their winter quarters.

Now the Federal soldiers ventured forth mainly on patrols and to find forage for their horses and mules. But a big reconnaissance in force, on December 20, led to the sharpest fighting since Ball's Bluff two months before. Two units of about brigade strength stumbled into each other at Dranesville, Virginia, just 12 miles down the Potomac from Ball's Bluff. A spirited fight followed and the Federals got the better of it, inflicting nearly three times more casualties than their own loss of 66 men killed and wounded. Among the beaten Confederates was one who would rarely taste defeat: Brigadier General J.E.B. Stuart.

Like Ball's Bluff, the affair at Dranesville was only an isolated incident. And there would be no other encounters for a while. For on the day of the clash, the commanding general of the Federal Army became seriously ill. Weakened by overwork, McClellan took to his bed with typhoid fever, and ru-

mors soon began circulating that his life was in danger. Lincoln went to visit McClellan, the first time he had called on the general since being snubbed five weeks before. This time the President was told that McClellan was too sick to see him, and was turned away at the door.

As 1861 came to a close, Lincoln was mired in gloom. The Union had been spending stupendous sums daily on the War, but there was little to show for it. The Federal armies both East and West seemed paralyzed. And now the general in chief was so ill that the President could not even talk with him.

The only bright spot was the resolution of the crisis caused back on November 8 when the U.S. Navy had seized the British steamer *Trent* on the high seas and taken into custody two Confederate emissaries to Europe. Throughout the North, the episode

Officers and men of the Army of the Potomac celebrate McClellan's appointment as general in chief with fireworks and a serenade in front of his Washington home in November 1861. McClellan came out on the balcony and bowed to the crowd but refused to make a speech.

This was the Joint Committee on the Conduct of the War. The seven-member body was called into being by Congress early in December, ostensibly to investigate the Federal failures at Bull Run and Ball's Bluff. But in fact the committee had the broadest possible mandate to inquire into "the conduct of the present war."

Radical Republicans controlled the Joint Committee. The chairman, Ohio Senator Benjamin Franklin Wade, was, in plain fact, a zealot—intensely partisan, harshly vindictive toward the South, and perfectly willing to ride roughshod over the Constitutional rights of witnesses who were haled before his committee.

Under Wade's aggressive leadership, the Joint Committee conducted its hearings in secret (then leaked to the press its own version of testimony), refused to allow witnesses legal counsel and took as gospel the wildest allegations of treasonous behavior. The President himself eventually had to endure the indignity of the committee's inquisition, appearing before it to deny rumors that his wife, Mary, who had a number of relatives in the Confederate Army, was—as the saying went—"two thirds slavery and the other third secesh."

The principal targets of the Joint Committee were Federal generals, especially West Pointers, who were Democrats or were considered insufficiently opposed to slavery. McClellan was the ranking suspect on both those counts, though on the flimsiest of evidence. For example, McClellan was thought to be lenient toward slavery because he saw the restoration of the Union, not emancipation, as the main purpose of the War—just as Abraham Lincoln did.

With McClellan ill, the Joint Committee

inflamed jingoistic passions and fears of British intervention on the Confederate side. However, Lincoln had released the two Confederates on Christmas Day, defusing the diplomatic crisis.

This practical move seemed to many just one more example of Lincoln's weakness. Attorney General Edward Bates, who admired Lincoln, lamented in his diary that "he lacks *will* and *purpose.*" Less friendly Republicans also perceived a lack of purpose in the President and resolved to put some backbone in the administration. These men were the so-called Radicals—senators and representatives who wanted to wage a swift and ruthless war against the Confederacy and to proclaim the emancipation of the slaves immediately. The Radicals had been nipping at Lincoln's flanks ever since Bull Run; now they forged a powerful new instrument for influencing military policy.

A burial detail, with drummers beating a slow march, lays to rest a Vermont soldier who died of illness at Camp Griffin, near Washington. Communicable diseases ravaged the training camps, striking hardest at new recruits. It was not uncommon for volunteer regiments to have one third of their men on sick list.

grilled his subordinates for any evidence that could be used against him. By the first week of 1862, Wade and his colleagues felt they had amassed enough proof of McClellan's alleged incompetence, if not of treasonable acts, to make an appeal to the President. On the night of January 6, they met with Lincoln and the Cabinet and demanded that Lincoln order McClellan to advance. In this and subsequent meetings with the Joint Committee, Lincoln defended his general in chief. But he was increasingly troubled by McClellan's strange inertia.

With McClellan still away from the scene, the President was urged by Attorney General Bates to "act out the powers of his place, to command the commanders." Lincoln in effect took over the job of general in chief. He telegraphed his commanders in the West—Henry Halleck in Missouri and Don Carlos Buell in Kentucky—directing them to coordinate their efforts and, above all, to move against the enemy. In fact, very little could be done in winter: Roads were impassable and equipment was unable to stand up to the extremes of weather. Nevertheless, Lincoln admonished the two generals, "Delay is ruining us, and it is indispensable for me to have something definite." The President confided to a friend that he was even "thinking of taking the field himself."

Lincoln quickly learned that being general in chief consisted of more than merely egging on his commanders. Word came back from the commanders in the West that neither felt his forces were large enough to wage an offensive. "It is exceedingly discouraging," Lincoln wrote on the back of the letter from Halleck. "As everywhere else, nothing can be done."

That day, January 10, Lincoln went in despair to the office of his able Quartermaster General, Montgomery C. Meigs. He slumped into a chair in front of the open fire and stared at the flames. "General, what shall I do? The people are impatient; Chase has no money and tells me he can raise no more; the General of the Army has typhoid fever. The bottom is out of the tub. What shall I do?"

Meigs pointed out that McClellan already had been in bed for three weeks and might well be incapacitated for three weeks more. He warned Lincoln that the enemy might attack during this period, and suggested that the President should therefore think about someone to replace McClellan as commander of the Army of the Potomac.

At Meigs's suggestion, Lincoln quickly convened a White House conference with several Cabinet members and two of McClellan's division commanders, Generals Irvin McDowell and William B. Franklin. "If General McClellan does not want to use the Army, I would like to *borrow* it," the President announced, "provided I could see how it could be made to do something."

Then Lincoln turned for ideas to the generals. McDowell, who had led the defeated Federal forces at Bull Run the previous July, called for another overland offensive against the Confederates in northern Virginia. Franklin, a confidant of McClellan's, proposed something approximating the Urbanna plan—an amphibious operation aimed at Richmond.

These two approaches were debated in subsequent sessions at the White House. George McClellan got wind that something was going on behind his back, struggled out of his sickbed and showed up at the White House looking pale, thin and angry. "My unexpected appearance," he noted later with satisfaction, "caused very much the effect of a shell in a powder magazine."

McClellan sat silent through most of the meeting on January 13. When the Secretary of the Treasury, Salmon Chase, challenged him to reveal his plans, the general refused. Some of those present "were incompetent to form a valuable opinion," he said, "and others incapable of keeping a secret." McClellan did indicate that he had fixed a schedule for an advance against the enemy, but he did not say what it was. At that, Lincoln—relieved that McClellan was back in the saddle—adjourned the meeting. But the general had made a powerful enemy of Chase, and had also irritated Seward, Meigs and Postmaster General Montgomery Blair.

Shortly afterward, McClellan was summoned before the Joint Committee. During the six-hour session, the general treated the committee members with impatience and barely disguised contempt. To some degree, his irritation was justified, although hardly diplomatic. For example, when the interrogation turned to McClellan's reasons for putting off an attack, he carefully explained the normal military procedure of securing a safe route of retreat before attempting to mount an offensive. Senator Zachariah Chandler misconstrued the explanation along partisan lines. After the general departed, Chandler turned to Chairman Wade and remarked, "I don't know much about War, but it seems to me that this is infernal unmitigated cowardice."

Since McClellan still had Lincoln's support, the Joint Committee went after one of his subordinates, Brigadier General Charles Stone. As the field commander at the Ball's

Atop Federal Hill, rising 82 feet above tidewater in south Baltimore, Federal soldiers stand guard at siege guns, which command Baltimore harbor and much of the city below.

On September 12, 1861, the 5th New York parades through the streets of Baltimore in its Zouave finery: red fez, white turban and leggings, blue jacket and baggy red pants.

Baltimore under the Occupier's Rule

Baltimore, a hotbed of Confederate sympathy in a border state, had become an occupied city in April of 1861. In quick reaction to pro-Southern riots, Federal soldiers arrived to garrison the local forts and to guard the railroads against sabotage. At first, the city's secessionists showed their hostility by heckling the troops and labeling them "Lincoln's hirelings." Gradually, however, familiarity bred tolerance.

The main force behind this changing attitude was the 5th New York Volunteers, generally called Duryée's Zouaves after their leader, Colonel Abram Duryée. The townspeople admired the regiment of Zouaves for their colorful uniforms, for their flashy parades through the city streets, even for their intimidating bayonet drills. Private Alfred Davenport, who became the unit's historian, wrote that the citizens showed the Zouaves "a great deal of respect" and, eventually, no small measure of affection.

Before leaving Baltimore, the 5th organized a "Grand Farewell Festival" for the townspeople, with the soldiers presenting songs, tumbling acts and dramatic readings. When the men embarked for the Peninsula on March 30, 1862, onlookers wept. "Eight months before they had made their entrance among strangers, with the mailed hand," wrote Davenport. "They were now taking their departure as friends."

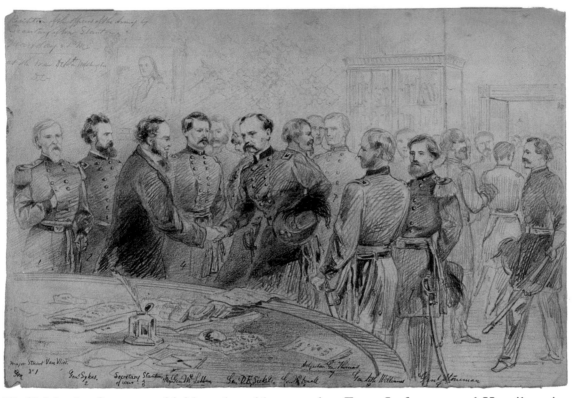

Secretary of War Edwin Stanton, standing beside General McClellan, shakes hands with an old client, Brigadier General Daniel E. Sickles, at a War Department reception in January 1862. In a lurid trial in 1859, defense attorney Stanton had won acquittal for Sickles, then a New York City Congressman charged with murdering his wife's lover.

Bluff debacle, Stone was highly vulnerable and a convenient scapegoat. In the committee hearings, vague testimony suggested that he was a Southern sympathizer. Some of Stone's officers alleged that just before Ball's Bluff a mysterious conference with Confederate officers was held under a flag of truce, and that messages had passed to and from Confederate officers across the upper Potomac in the sector of Stone's division. None of these allegations were ever proved, but that fact did not help Stone.

Stone appeared before the committee in January but failed to establish an adequate defense—mainly because he was never told the specific nature of the testimony against him. A few weeks later, at midnight on February 8, Stone was arrested by a detachment of Army troops. Though no formal charges were ever filed, he spent 189 days impris-

oned at Forts Lafayette and Hamilton in New York Harbor.

The official who ordered the arrest of General Stone was a new political power whose rise coincided with McClellan's illness. He was Edwin McMasters Stanton, who had recently replaced Simon Cameron as Secretary of War. Cameron had presided over a department so inept and corrupt that its transgressions—mainly favoritism in awarding contracts that resulted in the purchase of inferior cloth, spoiled pork and inoperable guns—filled 1,109 pages in a Congressional report.

Stanton, on the other hand, was an energetic administrator, personally incorruptible but possessed of an uncontrollable passion for intrigue. A former corporation lawyer, he had proved his ability and acumen as Attorney General in the last months of the Buchanan administration and as legal counsel under Cameron. Stanton took the department by storm, often transacting business for 18 hours a day. A gnomelike man of 47 years with thick chest, short legs and massive head, he would stand at his high desk like a captain on the poop deck, banging the desk top and calling out orders in a voice that sometimes rose to a hysterical screech. He intimidated practically everyone. "Don't send me to Stanton to ask favors," John Hay begged Lincoln's second private secretary, John Nicolay. "I would rather make a tour of a smallpox hospital."

At the very least, there was something

Brigadier General Charles P. Stone, the scapegoat for the Federal debacle at Ball's Bluff, asked for a court of inquiry, at which officers rather than politicians could judge his conduct. In denying the request, a staff officer candidly explained, "Your military superiors are under attack, and that consideration involves the propriety of abstaining just now."

odd about Stanton. As a boy in Ohio, he once terrified neighbors by walking into their home with two large snakes wriggling around his neck; he loved to train the creatures. As a man, he kept in his room a small metal box containing the ashes of a daughter who died in childhood. Some people in Washington thought he was demented.

But as a politician, Stanton was brilliant, albeit devious and unpredictable. He was a longtime Democrat, yet he managed to ingratiate himself with the most radical of the Republicans. Formerly a severe critic of Lincoln, Stanton quickly became one of the President's closest advisers. Lincoln admired Stanton's energy, his willingness to make hard decisions and his single-minded devotion to winning the War.

In appointing Stanton, Lincoln had assumed that the new Secretary would get along well with his general in chief. McClellan thought so too; he considered Stanton a friend and called his appointment "a most unexpected piece of good fortune." Indeed, it had been the conniving Stanton who had roused McClellan from his sickbed by telling him that Lincoln and the general's subordinates were conspiring against him.

But Stanton had no sooner moved into his new post than he changed positions and political coloration. Now he became inaccessible to McClellan and was making such declarations as, "The champagne and oysters on the Potomac must be stopped," and "I will force this man McClellan to fight."

Stanton's order to arrest General Stone, issued on January 28, was a clear sign that the Secretary was now in league with the Radicals of the Joint Committee. Lincoln winced at the order, saying that he was glad he "knew nothing of it until it was done."

McClellan sat on the order for 12 days and then reluctantly had his provost marshal take Stone into custody.

Though Stone's incarceration was intended partly to spur McClellan to action against the Confederates, it had the opposite effect. It made him more cautious, for McClellan saw Stone's humiliation as an object lesson. A similar fate might await McClellan if he committed the Army of the Potomac to a losing battle. He must make no move until he felt absolutely certain of victory.

Meanwhile, however, Lincoln decided he could wait no longer for McClellan. His patience exhausted, the President took an unprecedented step. On January 27, without consulting anyone, he decreed that by February 22, less than a month hence, there would be "a general movement of the land and naval forces of the United States against the insurgent forces." Four days later, Lincoln added another order, telling McClellan precisely what to do with the Army of the Potomac. The general was to attack the Confederates in northern Virginia at a point on the Orange & Alexandria Railroad southwest of Manassas Junction.

No United States President ever had taken so literally the title commander in chief, and Lincoln later confessed that it was "all wrong" to intervene so directly in military operations. But Lincoln's amateurish orders

had a salutary effect on McClellan. Faced with the order to move against Manassas, he was at last compelled to take the President into his confidence and explain in detail the Urbanna plan, which had been incubating for nearly three months. On February 3, he completed a 22-page letter comparing the two plans—his and Lincoln's—and concluding that his was the better. With the Urbanna approach, he said, "I regard success as certain by all the chances of war."

Lincoln was not wholly persuaded by McClellan's arguments. He feared that the Urbanna plan, by removing the bulk of the army from in front of Washington, might open up the capital to a sudden offensive by the Confederates in northern Virginia. This concern, very natural but usually groundless, was to bedevil Lincoln and his Cabinet throughout the War.

Nonetheless, Lincoln felt he either had to fire McClellan, which he was not prepared to do, or go along with the general's plan. Without revoking his two attack orders, Lincoln quietly let them lapse.

During the month of February, while McClellan waited for Lincoln to endorse the Urbanna plan and agree to chartering the necessary fleet of vessels, the clamor for a Virginia offensive continued to rise in the press, in Congress and in the Joint Committee on the Conduct of the War. The

A sprawl of Federal stables in snow-dusted Alexandria, Virginia, shelters horses and mules shipped south for the Army of the Potomac. More than 14,500 animals were on hand by April of 1862 for the beginning of the Peninsular Campaign.

pressure was further increased by Federal victories elsewhere, in operations that McClellan had proposed and encouraged as general in chief. In the sounds off North Carolina, a large amphibious expedition under the command of Brigadier General Ambrose E. Burnside reached Roanoke Island and defeated the Confederate garrison. In Kentucky in January, the Confederates tried to surprise Brigadier General George H. Thomas at Mill Springs but instead were defeated soundly. And in northwestern Tennessee, an obscure 39-year-old general named Ulysses S. Grant led the capture of Forts Henry and Donelson, two major Confederate river bastions.

The dramatic contrast between the toughness of Grant, who had demanded the unconditional surrender of Fort Donelson, and the apparent timidity of McClellan was not lost on Edwin Stanton. In a transparent attempt to undermine McClellan in the public esteem, the Secretary of War on February 19 wrote the New York *Tribune:* "Battles are to be won, now, and by us, in the same and only manner that they were ever won by any people since the days of Joshua—by boldly pursuing and striking the foe."

In spite of his many troubles, McClellan took time to console another troubled man. On February 20, Lincoln's 11-year-old son, Willie, died of what the physician described as "bilious fever." The general wrote one of the tenderest messages of sympathy that the President received. In addition to offering his condolences, McClellan said, "You have been a kind true friend to me in the midst of the great cares and difficulties by which we have been surrounded during the past few months. Your confidence has upheld me when I should

otherwise have felt weak. I am pushing to prompt completion the measures of which we have spoken, and I beg that you will not allow military affairs to give you a moment's trouble."

The "measures" McClellan referred to were the long-neglected business of clearing the Confederate batteries along the lower Potomac and the reopening of the Baltimore & Ohio Railroad above Harpers Ferry. Under orders from Lincoln to settle these matters before mounting the Urbanna expedition, McClellan devised a two-pronged campaign to protect the flanks of Washington. On the lower Potomac, 4,000 troops commanded by Brigadier General Joseph Hooker were to cross the river by boat from Maryland and attack the Confederate guns near Evansport, Virginia. At the same time, a larger force would bridge the upper Potomac at Harpers Ferry, guard the rebuilding of the broken stretch of railway and then— to protect the Baltimore & Ohio from further attacks—march southwest to occupy Winchester, the northernmost Confederate outpost in the Shenandoah Valley. By staging these two forays simultaneously, McClellan hoped to prevent the Confederate army at Manassas from marshaling reinforcements at either point.

On the 26th of February, McClellan went up the Potomac to supervise the crossing at Harpers Ferry. Engineers quickly laid a pontoon bridge across the river, and the vanguard of his 23,000 troops marched over while bands played.

To cross the main body of troops, along with their artillery and baggage, McClellan had ordered the construction of a larger, more solid bridge. Mindful of the disaster at

"MASTERLY INACTIVITY," OR SIX MONTHS ON THE POTOMAC.

A Northern cartoon mocks Generals McClellan in Washington and Beauregard in Virginia for their inactivity. When the Confederates withdrew from the Manassas area in March of 1862, another Northern satirist crowed, "It was a contest of inertia and our side outsat the other!"

Ball's Bluff, he intended at all cost to secure his line of retreat. His engineers had assured him that the larger bridge could be built by lashing together big canal boats side by side.

The boats were brought up the Chesapeake and Ohio Canal the following morning, February 27. When they reached the lock that would allow them to enter the Potomac, the boats, which had been designed only for canal travel, were found to be six inches too wide to fit through. McClellan already had enough men across at Harpers Ferry to safeguard the rebuilding of the railroad, but he had to call off the scheduled march against Winchester. And, fearing that the Confederates might now feel free to rein-

force the batteries downriver, he canceled the planned crossing of the lower Potomac.

Official Washington was enraged to learn that two attacks had been canceled—and all because no one had bothered to find out that the boats were too wide for the exit lock at Harpers Ferry. This glaring oversight drew a bitter gibe from Treasury Secretary Chase; he said that the Winchester campaign had "died of lockjaw." And the bungling triggered a rare display of temper on the part of the President.

Earlier that day, Lincoln and Stanton had given McClellan a vote of confidence by authorizing the procurement of vessels for his Urbanna expedition. But when they heard the news from Harpers Ferry that night, they summoned McClellan's chief of staff, General Randolph Marcy. The President, as Marcy later telegraphed McClellan, WAS IN A HELL OF A RAGE.

"Why in the nation, General Marcy," Lincoln stormed, "couldn't the general have known whether a boat would go through that lock before spending a million dollars getting them there? I am no engineer, but it seems to me that if I wished to know whether a boat would go through a hole or lock, common sense would teach me to go and measure it. Everything seems to fail. The impression is daily gaining ground that the general does not intend to do anything."

Realizing that the President's patience with McClellan was sorely strained, the Joint Committee demanded that Lincoln force the general to fight or fire him. Lincoln considered the proposition soberly. "If I remove McClellan," he asked, "whom shall I put in command?"

"Well, anybody!" Senator Wade replied.

"Wade, anybody will do for you," the President said, "but not for me. I must have somebody. I must use the tool I have." But Lincoln's doubts about his general in chief continued to deepen.

That winter Lincoln had no corner on presidential frustration over the military situation. In Richmond, 100 miles to the south, Jefferson Davis also had to contend with balky commanders and a rising tide of impatience in Congress and the newspapers. But Davis was Lincoln's opposite in temperament and background, and he dealt with his problems in an entirely different manner.

Unlike his counterpart, Davis had been a professional soldier. He had graduated

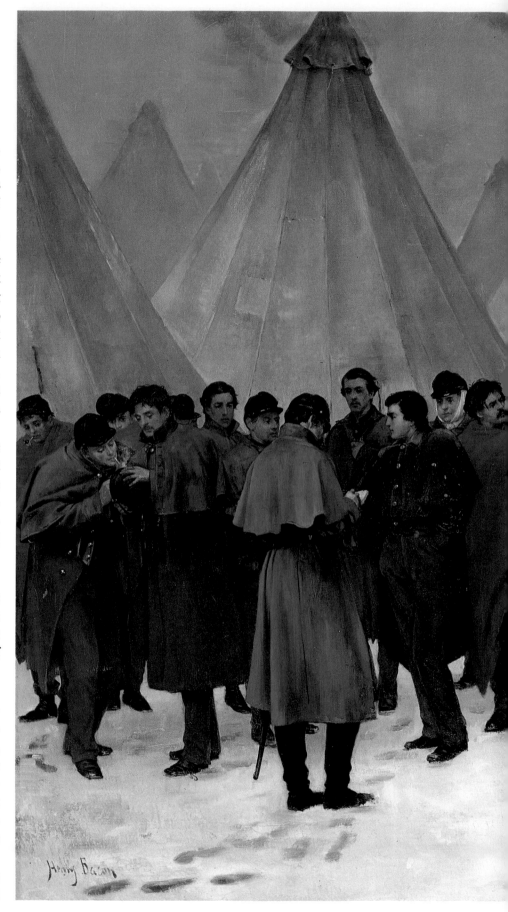

An officer *(left)* checks his company roster as soldiers of the Army of the Potomac fall in for morning roll call at a training camp outside Washington.

from West Point, served in the Black Hawk War, distinguished himself in the Mexican War as a regimental commander and later served as U.S. Secretary of War. Now he conducted military affairs as his own general in chief. It was Davis who, after the Confederacy's stunning victory at Bull Run the previous July, had mapped the Southern military strategy.

It was basically a defensive policy, stretching the Confederate forces, which already were outnumbered 2 to 1, across 3,500 miles of seacoast and another 1,400 miles of war front that extended from the Rio Grande to the Potomac. Davis felt that the defensive strategy was necessary for a number of reasons: The Confederacy was inferior in manpower and firepower; it was trying hard to persuade the rest of the world that it was merely defending itself against Union aggression; and it was committed to the principle of states' rights, which gave priority to meeting local demands for troops and impeded the concentration of forces needed to mount a large-scale offensive.

Some of Davis' disputes with his commanders in northern Virginia had stemmed from strategy. Two months after Bull Run, while McClellan was still in the early stages of building his army, Generals Joseph Johnston and P.G.T. Beauregard had asked for 20,000 additional men to mount an offensive from Manassas north across the Potomac, but Davis said he could not supply such reinforcements without "a total disregard of the safety of other threatened positions."

However, the clashes between Davis and the two generals had been caused less by disagreements over strategy than by irreconcilable conflicts of personality. Unlike Lincoln, who could shrug off a snub by his general

Confederate Secretary of War Judah P. Benjamin forged his friendship with Jefferson Davis by challenging him to a duel in 1858, when both men were U.S. Senators. Benjamin issued the challenge because Davis had falsely accused him of lying. West Pointer Davis, realizing that lawyer Benjamin knew little of weapons, was impressed by his courage and apologized on the Senate floor.

in chief, the Confederate President was, as a Richmond editor wrote, "ready for any quarrel with any and everybody, at any time and all times."

Davis found it easy to settle his disputes with Beauregard; he simply shunted the general westward, out of the limelight, to a front that was popularly regarded as less important than the East. But Davis' problems with Johnston ran deeper—dating back, rumor had it, to a fight over a woman when both were cadets at West Point. Johnston was 55 years old, a trim, jaunty man with a wedge-shaped face framed by sideburns, goatee and receding hairline; he was genial, generous with subordinates, as touchy as Davis when challenged and so highly regarded by military men that the President felt

Confederate General Joseph E. Johnston, a 32-year veteran of the U.S. Army, was renowned for his bravery fighting Indians and Mexicans. But his tendency to get wounded was so worrisome that as he left Richmond to take command on the Peninsula, General Robert E. Lee "held his hand a long time," an observer reported, "and admonished him to take care of his life."

constrained to treat him more cautiously than he had Beauregard.

Their differences were exacerbated when the President, in nominating five soldiers for the rank of full general, placed Johnston fourth on the seniority list even though the general had outranked all of the others in the prewar U.S. Army. Davis later tried to explain his action on the ground that Johnston had been a staff officer, not a line officer. It was obviously a lame excuse, for Davis had topped his list with a general, Samuel Cooper, who had also been a staff officer.

Of course the slight wounded Johnston's pride, and he wrote a nine-page letter to the President protesting the attempt "to tarnish my fair name as a soldier and a man." Davis' reply was brief and scathing: "I have just received and read your letter of the 12th instant. Its language is, as you say, unusual; its arguments and statements utterly one sided, and its insinuations as unfounded as they are unbecoming."

Through the rest of the autumn of 1861 and into the winter, Davis and Johnston bickered vigorously, often joined by Judah P. Benjamin, the recently appointed Secretary of War. Like his Northern counterpart, Edwin Stanton, Benjamin was a brilliant lawyer and former Attorney General with no military background but with a sharp tongue and a passion for order.

Since Johnston was a careless administrator, Benjamin—with Davis' backing—repeatedly involved himself in matters that Johnston felt were none of the Secretary's business. Intervention by Benjamin almost drove one of Johnston's top generals, Thomas J. Jackson, the man who had "stood like a stone wall" at Bull Run, to request reassignment to his former post as a professor at Vir-

In this rare, badly damaged photograph, men of the Texas Brigade prepare for a day of chores at their company mess, a log cabin jokingly named after their commanding officer. During the uneventful winter of 1861-1862, the Texans guarded a 10-mile stretch of the Potomac's Virginia shore.

ginia Military Institute—or even to resign from the Confederate Army entirely.

On the 19th of February, Johnston was summoned to a day-long strategy meeting with Davis and the Cabinet in Richmond. All of the news was bad. The recent fall of Roanoke Island on the North Carolina coast had opened up the possibility of a Federal attack against the important Confederate base at Norfolk, Virginia. In Tennessee, Davis' favorite general, Albert Sidney Johnston, was in full retreat after the loss of Forts Henry and Donelson. These reverses dimmed Confederate hopes for British recognition and Royal Navy help in breaking the Federal naval blockade.

General Johnston brought more bad news to the meeting. He said that his position around Manassas would soon become untenable. The good spring weather would dry the muddy roads and make it possible for McClellan to attack with superior forces. Johnston recommended a withdrawal to the south as soon as the roads were solid enough to bear artillery. How far south? asked Davis. Johnston said that he did not know yet because he was unfamiliar with the topography to his rear. Although Davis did not dispute the recommendation for withdrawal, he later called Johnston's ignorance of the terrain "inexplicable on any other theory than that he had neglected the primary duty of a commander."

Three days later, on the 22nd of February, even as Davis was gloomily taking the oath of office for his six-year term as the popularly elected President of the Confederacy, Johnston was taking steps at his Centreville headquarters that would deepen the President's despondency. Although no date had been set for the withdrawal from Manassas, Johnston already had decided that the sooner it was done the better. Two incidents had persuaded Johnston of the need to move quickly. After his meeting with Davis and the Cabinet, he had returned to his Richmond hotel only to find that the lobby was humming with word of his impending withdrawal from Manassas. Then, on the train back to Centreville, Johnston had run into an acquaintance who had heard the same talk even though, as Johnston noted, the man was "too deaf to hear conversation not intended for his ear."

That did it: If even the deaf knew that the withdrawal was imminent, McClellan would soon know it too and strike first. Johnston gave orders to begin shipping all surplus stores south. Since his government evidently could not keep a secret, he also decided not to tell the President of his plans.

Pulling out of the Manassas area was a prodigious task. Mountains of baggage had accumulated there—"A trunk had come with each volunteer," Johnston complained.

A shanty town of Confederate huts built as winter quarters during the fall of 1861 rises at Centreville, Virginia. The cabins were dank and crowded, spreading misery and disease.

Worse, over Johnston's protests, the Confederate commissary department had stockpiled twice the reserve rations he wanted and had even built a meat-packing plant at Thoroughfare Gap, northwest of Manassas, where more than two million pounds of bacon and salt beef were now piled up dangerously close to enemy lines.

Because horse-drawn wagons soon bogged down in the winter mud, Johnston had to rely on the Orange & Alexandria Railroad to move nearly everything south. The railroad had only a single track and practically no sidings, and traffic soon became so snarled that some trains required 36 hours to crawl the 60 miles from Manassas south to the junction at Gordonsville.

Johnston kept complaining to Richmond about conditions at Manassas—the mud, the "evil" stockpiling of stores, the "wretched" civilian management of the railroad—but not once did he make it clear to Davis that he was pulling out. Completely unaware, Davis meanwhile was writing Johnston urging him in the event of an evacuation to save as much matériel as possible, especially the precious heavy guns, even if it meant a delay.

Davis' letter had absolutely no effect on Johnston. Every report of Federal activity—the abortive attempt of February 27 to bridge the Potomac and march on Winchester, suspicious maneuvers by the Federals along the lower Potomac—persuaded Johnston that McClellan knew of his preparations and would outflank the Confederates before they could get out.

On March 7, Johnston ordered all of his troops east of the Blue Ridge Mountains—42,000 effectives—to fall back to the Rappahannock River, nearly halfway to Richmond. Only the 5,400 men under Major General Thomas J. Jackson in the Shenandoah Valley were exempt from the orders; they were to remain at their positions around Winchester as a threat to the right flank of any Federal advance.

By the evening of Sunday, March 9, the last of Johnston's infantry had evacuated their entrenchments at Manassas. Most of the heavy fortress guns along the Confederate front were left behind, some spiked but many still in working order. Rearguard cavalry stayed on to put the torch to rail cars, storehouses and the million pounds of meat still remaining at Thoroughfare Gap after local farmers had carted off everything they could. Johnston even made the supreme sacrifice and destroyed barrels of "medicinal" whiskey.

The smell of burning bacon allegedly provided Federal scouts with one of the first signs of the Confederate retreat. Until that Sunday evening, McClellan—contrary to Johnston's apprehensions—had no idea that the Confederate army was rapidly evacuating northern Virginia.

At that, the Union's general in chief was better informed than the Confederate President. The next day, March 10, Jefferson Davis was still so ignorant of Johnston's plans that he telegraphed the general, promising him reinforcements for Manassas and even suggesting an offensive to be launched from there as soon as the roads dried.

Johnston did not receive the wire, of course. He was en route south to the Rappahannock where, three days later, he would finally get around to informing Davis that his army was establishing a new line of defense.

"Stride of a Giant"

"The march up the Peninsula seemed very slow, yet it was impossible to increase our speed. I learned that it is so much easier to maneuver and fight around the corner grocery, than to fight, march and maneuver in mud and rain, in the face of a brave and vigilant enemy."

PRIVATE WARREN LEE GOSS, U.S. ENGINEER CORPS

For George McClellan, the startling news of the Confederate withdrawal from northern Virginia marked the culmination of an extraordinary week—turbulent days filled with such sudden shocks and reverses that everyone and everything seemed to be conspiring against him, not only the Confederates and his political enemies but fate itself.

McClellan had been disheartened after the abortive attempt to squeeze canal boats through narrow locks at Harpers Ferry on February 27 spoiled his planned assault on Winchester. Three days later, one of his favorite generals, Frederick W. Lander, died in western Virginia of what was diagnosed as a "congestive chill," but was actually pneumonia. At the funeral, McClellan was feeling so downcast that he told a colleague he almost wished he were in the coffin in place of Lander.

Then came a weekend of racking blows. In a meeting, Lincoln chastised McClellan for the failure at Harpers Ferry. This rebuke stunned the general, for Secretary of War Stanton had told him that the President was "fully satisfied." Then, according to McClellan's account, the President, who nine days earlier had approved the chartering of transports, allowed that he was having second thoughts about the general's plan to attack Richmond by way of a waterborne landing at Urbanna. People had been telling him, said Lincoln, that the whole thing was a treasonous plot to remove the Army of the

Potomac from in front of Washington and thus leave the nation's capital at the mercy of the Confederates.

Stung by the charge, McClellan sprang to his feet in protest and demanded an apology. Lincoln assured him that he did not believe the charge, but McClellan vowed to support his view that the Urbanna plan was a sound one. He hurried back to headquarters and gathered his 12 division commanders for a vote. He returned to the White House that afternoon, generals in tow, to announce the results: eight to four in favor of the Urbanna plan.

Just when that matter seemed to be settled satisfactorily, two peremptory General War Orders from the President were dropped on McClellan's desk. One order formally approved the Urbanna plan but set certain conditions: McClellan must leave the defenses of Washington "entirely secure"; he must obtain the agreement of his senior officers on the number of men to be left behind; he must move no more than half his force until the Confederate blockade of the lower Potomac was lifted; and the Army of the Potomac had to get moving within the next 10 days.

This order, McClellan felt, was an unwarranted infringement on his authority. And the second order he found even more offensive. It grouped the 12 divisions of the Army of the Potomac into four corps and designated four senior generals—Irvin McDowell, Edwin V. Sumner, Samuel P. Heintzelman

A so-called Quaker gun—a log carved, mounted and painted black to resemble a cannon—guards an abandoned Confederate fortification near Centreville, Virginia. The retreating Confederates left the dummy artillery behind to delay the Federals' pursuit.

and Erasmus D. Keyes—as commanders of the new units. McClellan did not oppose the corps idea, and he had discussed it with Lincoln some weeks before. But he had told the President that he wanted to wait until his generals could be tested in combat before selecting the corps commanders. Not only had McClellan been denied his request to appoint subordinates of his own choice, but three of the four senior generals chosen for him—Sumner, McDowell and Heintzelman—had cast votes against the Urbanna plan. McClellan feared their appointment doomed his strategy.

The following morning, Sunday, the 9th of March, word reached Washington of another threat to McClellan's planned advance on Richmond. At Norfolk, the Confederates had salvaged an old wooden frigate, the U.S.S. *Merrimac*, equipped her with armor and ten guns, renamed her the *Virginia* and sent her out to attack Federal warships in a vital waterway off Chesapeake

Bay called Hampton Roads. With the Confederate ironclad on the rampage, McClellan dared not send his Urbanna-bound invasion fleet into Chesapeake Bay. This concern was eased at 6:45 p.m., when the telegraph clicked out the latest from Hampton Roads: The new Federal ironclad *Monitor* had engaged the *Virginia* in an epic battle and had fought her to a draw.

Yet there was no respite for McClellan. As he conferred that evening with Lincoln and Stanton, word came confirming earlier reports of the Confederate pullout from Centreville and Manassas. The President's private secretaries, John Hay and John Nicolay (neither of whom was a friend to McClellan), reported that the general took the news "with incredulity which at last gave way to stupefaction."

McClellan hurried across the Potomac to prepare his army for the pursuit of the withdrawing Confederates. He recognized the irony of chasing an army that he had considered too strong to attack all winter; it was "a fool's errand," according to the harsh judgment of Attorney General Edward Bates. But McClellan had no choice. There was still the possibility of catching the Confederate rear guard.

At daylight on Monday, March 10, endless columns of Federal troops crossed the Potomac and joined others streaming out of camps on the Virginia side of the river. When the men reached Centreville and Ma-

nassas, there were no Confederates to fight, just abandoned entrenchments, smoldering supplies, and a few Quaker guns, logs left as props to confuse the Federals and retard their advance.

Newspaper reporters who accompanied the march pointed out with some relish that the empty enemy camps could have accommodated no more than half of the 150,000 Confederates McClellan had thought were entrenched there. A correspondent from the

WILLIAM F. SMITH   WILLIAM B. FRANKLIN   SAMUEL P. HEINTZELMAN   ANDREW PORTER   IRVIN MCDOWELL

General George B. McClellan, commander of the Army of the Potomac, stands for this photo with his senior generals prior to the Peninsular Campaign. All of the officers except McDowell, Buell and Blenker would serve with McClellan on the Peninsula during the army's advance on Richmond.

New York *Tribune* datelined his dispatch "Camp Disappointment, near Centreville."

To cap McClellan's distressing week, he received the flabbergasting news he was no longer general in chief of the Federal armies. Worse, the announcement was handled in a way that could not have been more offensive to him. Friends in Washington read of his demotion in the newspapers and telegraphed word to McClellan at his field headquarters at Fairfax Court House. Official notifica-

tion, conveyed by a presidential courier, arrived only later.

Lincoln justified the demotion on the ground that McClellan, "having personally taken the field" with the Army of the Potomac, could not devote the necessary attention to other battle fronts. That was true. But it was also true that the decision would not have been made without the maneuvering of Stanton and the Radicals, who were determined to show McClellan that the Sec-

GEORGE B. MCCLELLAN   GEORGE A. MCCALL   DON CARLOS BUELL   LOUIS BLENKER   SILAS CASEY   FITZ-JOHN PORTER

Federal soldiers manhandle a limber and a fieldpiece into place on board a transport docked at Alexandria in March 1862. McClellan's army took 260 cannon down Chesapeake Bay for the drive up the Peninsula.

retary of War was his superior. In any event, the commanders of all the Federal armies were ordered to report thenceforth to the Secretary of War.

Stanton, having acted to depose his erstwhile friend from one job, was also scheming to dislodge him as commander of the Army of the Potomac. While McClellan was at Manassas, Stanton brought to Washington as a possible successor Ethan Allen Hitchcock, a retired 64-year-old West Pointer named after his grandfather, the Revolutionary War hero. By his own admission, Hitchcock was a strange choice. He considered himself a "scholar rather than a warrior," was interested in mysticism and philosophy, and had written books about Jesus, Swedenborg and alchemy. Moreover, he was in poor health. Hitchcock quickly rejected Stanton's suggestion that he replace McClellan. He did agree to serve as a military adviser to the Secretary of War.

McClellan, unaware of Stanton's machinations, accepted his demotion with surprising equanimity. He wrote the President: "I shall work just as cheerfully as before."

His main concern at the moment was what to do with his army. An advance much beyond Manassas seemed to be out of the question. In their retreat to the south bank of the Rappahannock, the Confederates had burned a dozen or more bridges behind them. And the streams were so swollen and the roads so muddy that a large body of Federal cavalry sent to challenge the Confederate rear guard had to turn back exhausted before getting much more than halfway to the Rappahannock.

McClellan now recognized that his long-cherished Urbanna plan was no longer practical, even if he had had the authority to act

upon it. General Johnston's retreat had frustrated McClellan's design to outflank the Confederates. Indeed, Johnston's new line south of the Rappahannock put him in good position to thwart a landing at Urbanna. McClellan still did not want to march due south to Richmond, a move that surely would bring on several full-scale battles. He had to try some other tactic to avoid the Confederates' main strength.

After a day of solitary thinking, the general presented to his four new corps commanders another scheme, though not a new one. He had offered it up the previous month as an alternative to the Urbanna plan.

This plan also called for an amphibious expedition. The army would sail past Urbanna, continue down Chesapeake Bay and land at the tip of the Virginia Peninsula, that tongue of history-rich land framed by the York and James Rivers. There old Fort Monroe, which had been held by the Federals despite their loss of Norfolk just three miles across Hampton Roads, would serve as a secure base for the march up the Peninsula to Richmond.

Fort Monroe was about 70 miles southeast of Richmond—a distance 10 miles shorter than the route from Manassas. It had other presumed advantages. McClellan had been told that the roads on the Peninsula were passable at all seasons of the year. In addition, though the C.S.S. *Virginia* had the James River bottled up on the southern side of the Peninsula, McClellan was counting upon the Federal navy for support on the York River to the north.

The four corps commanders endorsed the Peninsula plan unanimously, but with several conditions. Most notably, the Navy must guarantee full cooperation around the Penin-

McClellan's army landed at Fort Monroe and in April began its advance up the Peninsula, clashing with the Confederates at Burnt Chimneys, laying siege to Yorktown and fighting battles at Williamsburg and Hanover Court House. By the end of May, the Federals were only six miles from Richmond. But then Johnston's Confederate army struck back with a massive attack at Seven Pines.

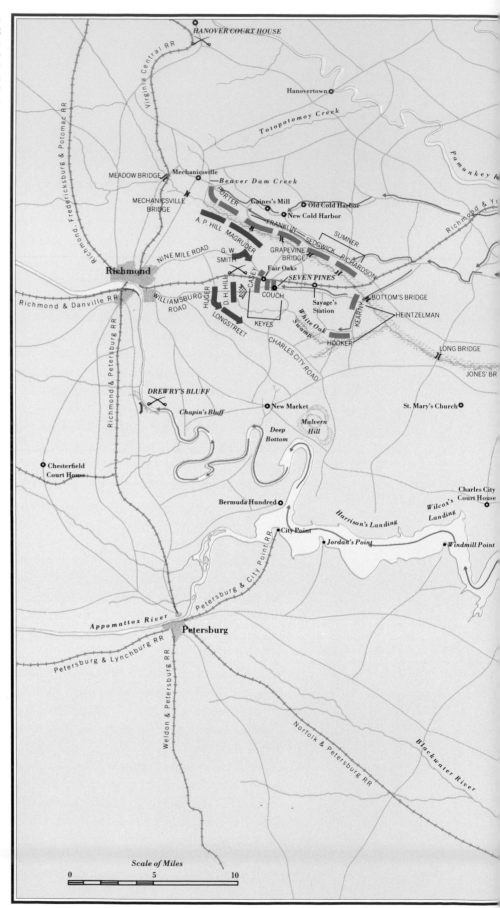

sula, and enough troops must be left to the defense of Washington to give the capital "an entire feeling of security."

McClellan agreed, and with his political flanks thus covered—after all, these were administration-appointed generals who had endorsed his plan—he won approval from the President. Then McClellan marched the main body of his army back to Alexandria on the Virginia side of the Potomac. There scores of ships of every description, from oceangoing vessels and river steamers to barges and tugs, had already assembled for the defunct Urbanna plan.

McClellan's spirits soared. He felt that he was again in the good graces of the President, whom he called "my strongest friend." And he welcomed the task of mounting the expedition to Fort Monroe, which gave him the opportunity to demonstrate his unquestioned abilities as an organizer. Riding to and fro on his mount, Dan Webster, he reveled in the tedious details of moving by ship well over 100,000 men and all their impedimenta.

On Monday, March 17, only a week after the embarrassing march to Manassas, the first of McClellan's divisions embarked at Alexandria—one day ahead of the deadline imposed by the President. "The worst is over," the general reassured Stanton by letter. "Rely upon it that I will carry this thing through handsomely."

During the following three weeks, nearly 400 vessels shuttled back and forth along the 200-mile route to Fort Monroe. The fleet transported 121,500 men, 14,592 animals, 1,150 wagons, 44 batteries of artillery and 74 ambulances, along with pontoon bridges, telegraph wire and everything else needed to sustain an army. In magnitude the

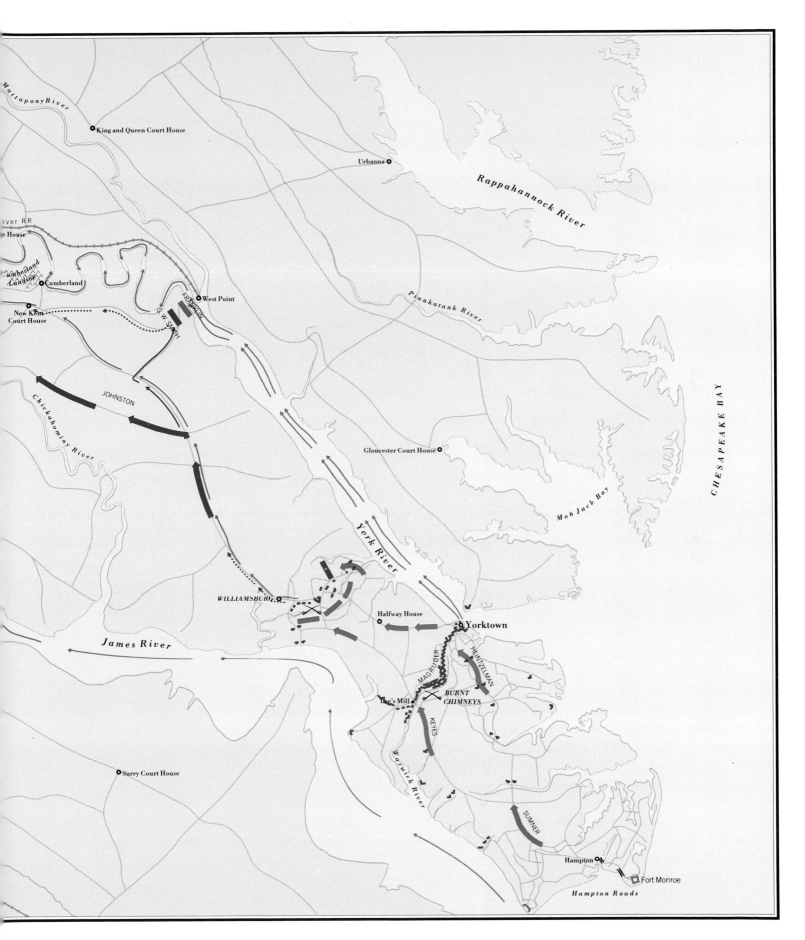

MATTAPONY RIVER

King and Queen Court House

Urbanna

RAPPAHANNOCK RIVER

River RR

e House

Cumberland
Landing

Cumberland

New Kent
Court House

FRANKLIN

West Point

G. W. SMITH

JOHNSTON

Chickahominy River

Piankatank River

CHESAPEAKE BAY

Gloucester Court House

York River

Moh Jack Bay

WILLIAMSBURG

Halfway House

Yorktown

James River

MAGRUDER

HEINTZELMAN

Lee's Mill

BURNT
CHIMNEYS

KEYES

Warwick River

Surry Court House

SUMNER

Hampton

Fort Monroe

Hampton Roads

91

A Confederate gun crew mans a cannon at Wynn's Mill, a dam along the Warwick River three miles south of Yorktown. Casualties at Yorktown were so few that a *Harper's Weekly* artist sketched this gun solely because it killed Lieutenant Orlando Wagner, a topographical engineer who was mapping the works for the Federals.

invasion force was probably without precedent, and its move toward Richmond was truly, as a British observer remarked, "the stride of a giant."

McClellan was delighted to have his grand venture finally under way. But even now an incident marred his happy prospect. The President was prevailed upon by the Radicals to establish a new department in western Virginia for their favorite general, John Charles Frémont, whom Lincoln had recently fired from overall command in the West. At the last minute—and "with great pain," Lincoln told McClellan—the President detached the 10,000-man division of General Louis Blenker from the Army of the Potomac and sent it off to Harpers Ferry to join Frémont's new army.

McClellan took the loss with good grace,

for Lincoln had offered assurance that no more troops would be taken from his command. Nonetheless, the general on April 1 was greatly relieved to board his steamer, the *Commodore*, and put out from the dock in Alexandria. Sailing down the Potomac that afternoon, he wrote his wife that he was glad to leave Washington—"that sink of iniquity."

The following afternoon, the 2nd of April, the *Commodore* anchored off Fort Monroe, and McClellan got his first glimpse of the battleground he had chosen. The Peninsula, about 50 miles long and nowhere more than 15 miles wide, was low, flat, sandy country, sparsely populated and heavily wooded and dissected with innumerable streams.

McClellan's plan was to move rapidly up the Peninsula and make his base near West

Point, at the head of the York River. Between West Point and Richmond, he expected "a decisive battle" to be fought.

The principal roadblock in the approach to West Point appeared to be at Yorktown, 20 miles up the York River from Fort Monroe. According to McClellan's best information, the Confederates had surrounded the town with earthworks, building upon the 80-year-old fortifications erected by the British during the Revolutionary War. Here and at Gloucester Point, 1,000 yards across the river, the Confederates reportedly maintained a garrison of about 15,000 men and had mounted heavy naval guns that commanded the approaches by both land and water.

To reduce the heavy batteries at Yorktown and Gloucester, McClellan was counting upon "a combined naval and land attack," with the Federal Navy concentrating all available warships in the assault. As soon as he arrived at the Peninsula, he visited the command ship of Flag Officer Louis M. Goldsborough to talk over plans. To McClellan's surprise, he learned that the Navy could not spare the gunboats; practically every warship in the area had been assigned to Hampton Roads to neutralize the *Virginia*. The Navy knew nothing of his plans for the gunboats. He would have to go ahead without them. (Navy officials said later that the gunboats would have been of little help in any case. The batteries at Yorktown and Gloucester were placed on bluffs too high for the gunboats' cannon to reach at their effective range.)

The following evening, April 3, McClellan got more bad news: Washington informed him that the 10,000-man garrison at Fort Monroe, which had been assigned to his army, was to be used for other purposes and would no longer be at his disposal. Nevertheless, the general still felt confident. That night he wrote his wife: "I hope to get possession of Yorktown day after tomorrow."

The next morning, without waiting for more troops and equipment still en route, he began his advance up the Peninsula in two long columns. The army's III Corps, under Brigadier General Samuel Heintzelman, headed up the road directly toward Yorktown. But IV Corps, under Brigadier General Erasmus Keyes, swung left, aiming to flank Yorktown by taking a place called Halfway House, four and a half miles beyond the Confederate bastion. Brigadier General Edwin Sumner's II Corps followed in reserve, on the main Yorktown road.

"It was a perfect Virginia day," a Federal soldier remembered. The sun shone, the grass was green and the peach trees were in bloom. The blue-clad columns marched a dozen miles, easily forcing the evacuation of the few scattered Confederate outposts. One position abandoned by the Confederates was Big Bethel, where Federal troops had been beaten on June 10, 1861, in the War's first battle on Virginia soil.

McClellan's troubles began the following morning, April 5. His maps were all wrong, failing to show the numerous muddy streams that slowed their progress. Clouds rolled in and rain came down in torrents. The roads, which McClellan had been told were passable at all times, turned to gumbo. Wagons sank up to their axles and, according to an officer's tall tale, a mule was swallowed up to its ears. (It was a *small* mule, the officer conceded.)

By early afternoon, Heintzelman's corps on the right drew up on the marshy ground in front of Yorktown and came under artillery and rifle fire. The town was enclosed by earthworks, and facing McClellan were parapets 15 feet thick fronted by ditches up to 10 feet deep and 15 feet wide.

McClellan had expected this. He was prepared to halt and trade long-distance cannon fire with the fort at Yorktown while his other column, under General Keyes, passed by well to the left of the Confederate defenses. But unknown to McClellan, Keyes's column was bogged down before an obstacle that was not supposed to be there—the Warwick River. According to the map, the Warwick flowed roughly parallel to the road Keyes and his troops had been following; in reality, the river cut directly across the Federals' path.

In its natural state the Warwick had been small and sluggish, not much of an obstacle. However, early settlers had built two mill dams across it, and in recent months the Confederates had constructed three more. These dams had widened and deepened the river behind them, and now it could be crossed easily only at the dams. Each dam was now guarded by artillery and riflemen dug in behind earthworks.

Keyes discovered all this shortly before noon that day, when he was greeted by rifle and artillery fire from the Confederate redoubt at Lee's Mill Dam, six miles from Yorktown and roughly in the middle of the Peninsula. After a quick reconnaissance, Keyes sent McClellan a cautionary message, warning him that "no part of the line, so far discovered, can be taken by assault without an enormous waste of human life."

McClellan received Keyes's disturbing dispatch in front of Yorktown late that afternoon. At the least, it meant a delay in turning the left flank of the Confederates at York-

Soldiers of the 61st New York warm themselves by a campfire outside Yorktown in this painting by Winslow Homer, who stayed with the regiment through the siege.

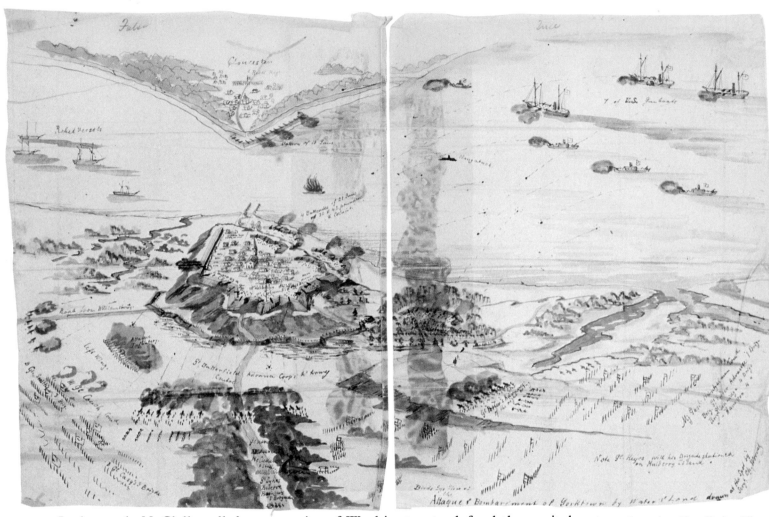

town. It also made McClellan all the more anxious for the arrival of his I Corps under Irvin McDowell. He had deliberately scheduled McDowell's seasoned command as the last to embark from Alexandria, for he planned to use its 38,000 men as reserves to throw into battle wherever they might be needed the most.

But I Corps would never arrive. While McClellan was listening to the cannonading at Yorktown, he was handed a telegram from the War Department. The President had denied McClellan the use of McDowell's corps, which was to remain in the vicin-

ity of Washington to defend the capital.

The safety of Washington, as McClellan knew, had been uppermost in the President's mind all along. Loss of the capital would undermine Union prestige abroad, probably bringing the Confederacy a great deal of foreign aid. Yet McClellan thought he had provided amply for Washington's safety. Just before leaving Alexandria, he had sent the War Department a table of units assigned to the protection of the capital. The units totaled more than 73,000 men—well beyond the 40,000 defenders considered necessary by his corps commanders.

A map drawn by a New York soldier depicts the Confederate stronghold of Yorktown besieged by Federal troops. Federal gunboats in the York River are under fire from the town and from Gloucester Point, just across the river.

There were discrepancies and mistakes in McClellan's arithmetic, however. He had counted some men twice, and he had included Blenker's division, which was now destined for western Virginia. What was more, nearly half the troops in the units listed were stationed 50 miles to the west of Washington in the Shenandoah Valley, a long way from the capital. McClellan still considered these men part of Washington's defenses, since the Shenandoah was the most likely route for any invasion by the Confederates; indeed, General Thomas J. Jackson was already stirring up trouble there. But McClellan had neglected to explain his reasoning to Lincoln.

After the general's departure for the Peninsula, the Radical Republicans began preying upon the President's concern for the security of Washington. The very day after McClellan left, Brigadier General James S. Wadsworth, a New York politician who had been appointed military governor of the District of Columbia, complained to Secretary of War Stanton that he had only 19,000 second-line troops available to man the forts around Washington.

Though Wadsworth added that an enemy attack was "very improbable," his complaint raised questions as to whether McClellan had fulfilled his charge to leave the capital "entirely secure." The Radicals and senior staff officers prodded Lincoln, and at last he agreed to divert the corps earmarked for McClellan to protect Washington.

At Yorktown, McClellan was angered and embittered by the news. The withdrawal of McDowell's corps was "the most infamous thing that history has recorded," he wrote his wife. It confirmed his growing suspicions that the Radicals were out to ruin him. In a week, more than a third of the 156,000-man force he had expected to have available had been taken away by presidential orders that seemed to be, at least in part, influenced by political rather than military considerations. To make matters worse, Stanton had inexplicably closed recruiting offices in the North, which surely would slow the build-up of Federal forces and make it more difficult for McClellan to replace the units withheld from him. Even some people who disliked McClellan sympathized with his plight. Back in Washington, Lincoln's secretary John Hay wrote in his diary: "McClellan is in danger, not in front but in rear."

All the same, McClellan was certainly powerful enough to have broken through the Confederate defenses that afternoon of April 5. He had 58,000 men in front of the Warwick River and nearly as many available at Yorktown or en route—facing a Confederate force he believed to number only about 15,000.

When would he attack? Lincoln, haunting the telegraph room at the War Department for news from the Peninsula and from Tennessee, where Ulysses S. Grant was heavily engaged at a place called Shiloh Church, waited impatiently for McClellan to take advantage of his overwhelming numerical superiority. Soon he telegraphed McClellan: I THINK YOU HAD BETTER BREAK THE ENEMY'S LINE FROM YORKTOWN TO WARWICK RIVER AT ONCE.

Still McClellan delayed. He bombarded Washington with pleas for more men, and decided that before assaulting the Warwick River defenses with infantry, he would conduct what he later called "the more tedious, but sure operations of siege."

One reason McClellan failed to mount an

Confederate earthworks 15 feet thick and a network of underground shelters called bombproofs defend the approaches to Yorktown. Sections of the defense line dated back to the American Revolution.

immediate assault was that the Confederates before him appeared to be receiving massive reinforcements. The Confederate commander, Major General John Bankhead Magruder, was no great soldier, but he had a flair for showmanship; in the prewar army he had relieved the tedium of garrison duty by producing and starring in amateur theatricals. And now, with a cast of 11,000 troops (4,000 fewer than Federal intelligence estimated), he staged a veritable extravaganza.

Magruder's artillery fired at anything in sight. After dark his bands played noisily. Along the Warwick River, where he had only 5,000 men to cover ten miles of front, a column of his men marched around in a circle, part of which lay in plain view of enemy outposts. For hours Federal observers watched the same few hundred gray-clad troops pass in endless review, emerging from a thicket, crossing a road, reentering the thicket and circling through it to reappear once more.

McClellan spared no effort to learn more about the Confederates' numbers and activities. He urged his commanders to make use of a new, untried instrument of reconnaissance—the observation balloons of aeronaut Thaddeus Lowe (pages 146-153). He himself scouted the Warwick River line, making personal reconnaissances that he admitted to his wife were "more appropriate to a lieutenant of engineers than to the commanding general."

Everything McClellan learned tended to increase his alarm. On April 7 he wrote, "The Warwick River grows worse the more you look at it." He wrote Lincoln: "It seems clear that I shall have the whole force of the enemy on my hands, probably not less than 100,000 men, and possibly more." In his reply, Lincoln questioned McClellan's arith-

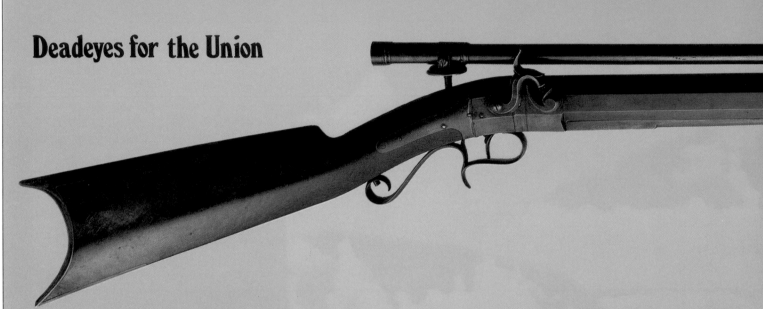

Deadeyes for the Union

COLONEL HIRAM BERDAN, 1ST U.S. SHARPSHOOTERS

No Federal unit that fought in the Peninsular Campaign drew more public attention than the 1st U.S. Sharpshooters, a band of rifle specialists who wore forest-green uniforms for camouflage. Organized in 1861 by Hiram Berdan, the nation's foremost marksman, the Sharpshooters mustered two regiments totaling nearly 2,000 volunteers—and every man a crack shot.

Before accepting a volunteer, Colonel Berdan required him to pass an exacting test: placing 10 consecutive shots inside a target 10 inches in diameter from a distance of 200 yards. It was no wonder that from their earliest battles, Berdan's experts performed remarkable feats with the rifle.

At Yorktown, an enterprising New Hampshire Sharpshooter, known to his fellows as Old Seth, crept into an empty Confederate rifle pit between the lines early one morning. From this advanced position, he was able to pick off the gunners of an enemy cannon. For the next two days, Seth's comrades kept him supplied with food and water, and Seth kept the cannon out of action.

Berdan's men were so accurate that inevitably their prowess was exaggerated. One fanciful tale concerned a small detachment of Sharpshooters at Yorktown who found themselves under heavy fire from a Confederate cannon. They noticed that the gun's muzzle was surrounded by sandbags, and aimed their shots so as to flick sand from the bags into the gun's muzzle. The cannon fired 12 more times—so the tale went—but on the 13th round, fouled by the sand, it blew up. The yarn fails to account for the fact that the Confederate gunners would have swabbed out the barrel—and any sand inside it—between rounds.

Soon newspapers were claiming that one of the Sharpshooters, Private Truman Head, or California Joe (*opposite*), a mild-mannered, keen-eyed hunter of grizzly bears, had "shot a man out of a tree two miles off, just at daybreak, first pop." A Confederate officer settled for the more modest estimate that Berdan's marksmen "rarely missed a man at a mile." In fact, this distance was about three times the Sharpshooters' effective range. In any case, one fact was quite clear: The Sharpshooters quickly obliged Confederate malingerers who hoped for a clean minor wound that would send them to safety in the rear. "It was only necessary," said one Confederate, "to hold up your hand to get a furlough."

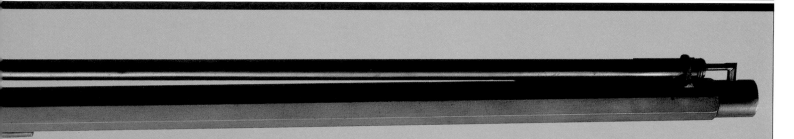

.45-CALIBER JAMES TARGET RIFLE
Equipped with a four-power telescopic sight, this 14-pound James target rifle delivered accurate fire up to 500 yards. Two companies of Berdan's Sharpshooters used this weapon and other types of heavy target rifles during the siege of Yorktown; those in other companies carried less accurate but lighter Colt repeating rifles, except for the marksman known as California Joe *(below)*, who preferred his own breech-loading Sharps.

California Joe of Berdan's Sharpshooters lies in wait for Confederate soldiers with his Sharps rifle.

metic. He also suggested that widespread impatience with McClellan's delays made it "indispensable to *you* that you strike a blow. *I* am powerless to help this."

Still McClellan hesitated, and not only because of his exaggerated view of Confederate strength. A siege of Yorktown—not an attack—had been in the back of his mind from the day he first planned the Peninsular Campaign. Seven years before, as an official U.S. military observer during the Crimean War, he had been fascinated by the great siege of Sevastopol. Siege warfare, with its slow, methodical operations, appealed to the engineer in McClellan, and to his native caution and earnest desire to save soldiers' lives.

Predictably, McClellan's long delay gave the Confederates time to fulfill his fears and send reinforcements to the Peninsula. And yet as late as April 16, the general had one last chance to win a quick victory by assault. He had only to take advantage of an unexpected stroke of good luck.

On the morning of the 16th, McClellan directed Brigadier General William F. Smith, commander of the 2nd Division, IV Corps, to conduct a reconnaissance in force at a place called Burnt Chimneys, a dam site one mile north of Lee's Mill in the middle of the Warwick River line. Two batteries of Federal artillery pounded the Confederate earthworks across the river, silencing two out of three of the Confederate guns covering the dam. Then Smith sent the Vermont Brigade—five regiments under Brigadier General William T. H. Brooks—forward to the edge of the Warwick. A staff officer found a fording place and two companies of the 3rd Vermont splashed across. Quickly the Vermonters drove the Confederates from their forward rifle pits. Then Brooks

sent three companies of the 4th Vermont on a charge over the mill dam, while four companies of the 6th Vermont crossed the river at the ford.

At this point, the Confederate river line had been broken. If McClellan, who arrived on the scene to observe, had thrown large numbers of troops across the river to hold open the breach, he could have sent the bulk of his army on through the gap toward Richmond, leaving Yorktown isolated in his rear to be taken at leisure. But McClellan was content to have captured good riverside positions for his artillery, and a glowing opportunity passed.

An hour after the operation started, reinforced Confederates under Brigadier General Howell Cobb counterattacked, killing 32 Vermonters. General Smith later reported the result: "The moment I found resistance serious and the numbers opposed great, I acted in obedience to the warning instructions of the general-in-chief, and withdrew the small number of troops exposed."

By the time the clash at Burnt Chimneys took place, Confederate reinforcements in substantial numbers were beginning to arrive on the Peninsula. For a while, Richmond had delayed in sending troops because McClellan's objective had not yet become obvious; his target might have been Norfolk, for example.

Even after McClellan's plans appeared clear, General Johnston was reluctant to furnish troops from his army, which by early April was encamped south of the Rappahannock and Rapidan Rivers, 50 miles northwest of Richmond. Johnston considered the Peninsula fortifications indefensible—easy prey for McClellan's big guns and susceptible to a flanking move up the York River. Instead of sharing his strength with Magruder, he preferred to concentrate all the available Confederate forces in front of Richmond and there fend off and destroy McClellan's invaders.

Jefferson Davis undertook to persuade Johnston to reinforce the Peninsula. To help him in this task the President now had a new high command. He had replaced the abrasive Secretary of War, Judah Benjamin, with George W. Randolph, who had served in both the Army and the Navy and was willing to confine himself to administrative duties. Davis also had appointed a military adviser, a kind of unofficial general in chief charged with "the conduct of military operations under the direction of the President." The adviser was Robert E. Lee, who, since turning down the command of the U.S. Army at the start of the War, had been working for the Confederacy in various minor capacities, most recently organizing coastal defenses in Georgia.

A Federal private and sergeant visit the graves of 3rd Vermont soldiers who were killed at Burnt Chimneys. The regiment bore the brunt of Federal losses in the hot little fight; of the four companies engaged, 23 men died and 51 were wounded.

Outside Yorktown, officers of the 1st Connecticut Heavy Artillery stand proudly beside their 13-inch seacoast mortars, 8½-ton monsters that could throw 220-pound shells 4,300 yards. The Federals laboriously brought up 14 batteries of heavy cannon for the siege, but the Confederates evacuated Yorktown before 13 of the units could fire a shot.

Lee's patience and tact made him the perfect intermediary between the thin-skinned Johnston and the prickly President. In direct opposition to Johnston, Lee believed that the narrow Peninsula afforded great advantages for an outnumbered defense force. And yet Lee dealt so diplomatically with Johnston that he was able to impose his strategy without serious discord. Starting on April 10, Johnston gradually shifted units from his army to the Peninsula.

On the 17th of April, the day after the small force of Vermonters briefly breached the center of the Warwick River line, Johnston himself arrived at Yorktown; he had just been appointed commander of troops on the Peninsula. By this time, all but two of the seven divisions in his army—now known as the Army of the Potomac, like McClellan's—had reached the Peninsula or were en route there.

In the next few days, Confederate strength under Johnston soared past 50,000 men. As the Federals' numerical superiority rapidly dwindled to less than 2 to 1, an infantry assault without a siege no longer seemed feasible, even for officers more aggressive than McClellan.

On April 22, in response to continuing entreaties to Washington, McClellan received a substantial part of McDowell's withheld corps—the 12,000-man division of Brigadier General William B. Franklin, one of his favorite generals. For a while, McClellan talked of using these men in an amphibious assault a few miles below Gloucester Point on the far side of the York River, but then he thought better of it and kept them aboard their transports to await completion of his siege preparations.

McClellan entrusted the siege operation to Brigadier General Fitz-John Porter, a capable West Pointer and a long-time friend who commanded the sole Regular Army division in the Army of the Potomac. Porter knew his job and did it thoroughly, even to the extent of ascending frequently in Thaddeus Lowe's balloons to study the enemy's dispositions. On one ascension, the balloon broke its mooring lines and drifted over enemy lines. When it finally drifted back to friendly territory, Porter climbed up in the rigging to open the gas valves and landed safely on top of a Federal tent.

The bombardment of Yorktown was to begin on May 5, and the preparations took time and enormous labor. To protect the big siege guns McClellan had brought with him, soldiers working under cover of night dug a line of earthworks paralleling the enemy line about a mile from it. Behind this parallel, ramps and platforms of logs and earth were erected.

The big guns could be brought up part of the way by barge on a creek branching from the York River. But then to convey them inland over knee-deep muck, logs had to be laid crosswise and great carts shipped in to carry the guns down the corduroy roads. The biggest cannon, seacoast Parrott guns that fired 200-pound shells, weighed more than 10 tons each and required teams of up to 100 horses to pull them. Then the guns had to be maneuvered onto their platforms by elaborate rigs of block and tackle. Other troops labored endlessly at fashioning defenses for the gun batteries and earthworks: gabions, or cylindrical baskets woven of twigs and filled with earth; bundles of closely bound wood known as fascines; and chevaux-de-frise, lengths of timber traversed with wooden spikes.

105

It was grueling, tedious work. Mosquitoes and fleas abounded. Two out of every three days it rained, and every hour or so the Confederate artillery would send over lethal greetings. But by Saturday, May 3, nearly all the siege guns were in place—114 of them in addition to the more than 300 pieces of smaller field artillery accompanying the army. Most of the big batteries were arrayed in front of Yorktown, where in the weakly fortified gap between Yorktown and the head of the Warwick River, McClellan intended to concentrate his infantry assault.

But Johnston had plans of his own. He decided to withdraw. Though he knew his old Mexican War comrade was overly cautious ("No one but McClellan could have hesitated to attack"), he understood that he could not compete with McClellan's big guns. Late that Saturday afternoon, to mask his intentions, Johnston's artillery sent up a terrific din. Then, after dark, the Confederates filed out of their soggy fortifications and began retreating up the Peninsula toward the old colonial capital, Williamsburg, 12 miles to the west.

The evacuation, which required several hours, was carried out with great stealth. In the Federal camp in front of Yorktown, McClellan was writing his wife shortly after midnight when he noted uneasily "the perfect quietness which reigns now." At daybreak it became apparent that the Confederates were gone. Thus, in the end, McClellan won Yorktown as he had always hoped to—without a fight.

Federal troops advancing cautiously into Yorktown that Sunday morning found 56 naval guns, which the Confederates had abandoned as too heavy to transport. And they found something more insidious. The

107

Kearney at Battle of Williamsburg

Brigadier General Philip Kearny, the one-armed Federal commander (*above*), leads the vanguard of his division against the Confederate defenses at Williamsburg (*left*). "He seemed to be ubiquitous," wrote a Confederate. "His striking manly form was present where the fighting was thickest."

Confederates had buried cannon shells attached to wire fuses that were activated by the weight of men or horses. These so-called torpedoes took several lives, and in angry reaction McClellan denounced the devices as "murderous and barbarous," and assigned Confederate prisoners of war the task of digging them up.

Partly because of the torpedoes, but mainly because the Confederate evacuation came as such a surprise, McClellan's cavalry did not start in pursuit until about noon, and it took even longer for five divisions of infantry to follow the horsemen up the Peninsula. But while muddy roads slowed the Federal horses, the progress of Johnston's weapons and artillery was even slower. The two Confederate columns—on the roads from Yorktown and from Lee's Mill in the mid-

dle of the Peninsula—averaged less than a mile an hour.

Finally in midafternoon, the Federal cavalry and horse artillery, under Brigadier General George Stoneman, caught up with Johnston's rearguard horsemen a few miles short of Williamsburg. After a series of running skirmishes, the Confederate cavalrymen took refuge behind a line of earthworks two miles east of town, where they were soon reinforced by several brigades of infantry that Johnston detached from his rear guard to check his pursuers. Well-aimed Confederate artillery fire soon drove back the pursuing horsemen.

The line of light fieldworks manned by the Confederates had been constructed by Magruder some months before. It consisted of 13 redoubts and extended for about four miles across the narrow neck of the Peninsula. Its flanks were impassable, blocked by creeks and marshes. The largest redoubt was Fort Magruder, an enormous bastion 600 yards wide that occupied the center of the line. Guns in the port commanded the point a mile away where the two roads up the Peninsula converged.

An open plain dotted with rifle pits extended from the fort. Beyond this plain and along the two converging roads lay a tangled stretch of logs, stumps and brush; the debris was left when part of the woods had been cut to give the defenders a clear field of fire and to build an obstructive abatis—a barricade of felled trees—to slow the attackers. This terrain was the setting for a rearguard action that grew into the first full-scale battle of the Peninsular Campaign.

Neither opposing commander had anticipated the Battle of Williamsburg, and neither was there when it began. McClellan had stayed behind near Yorktown to supervise the embarkation of four divisions; these units he sent 30 miles up the York River to West Point in hopes of cutting off the Confederate retreat. But Johnston, who suspected just such a flanking move by McClellan, was already beyond Williamsburg, his column hurrying to get safely past the West Point area.

The day of the battle, May 5, was miserable, with torrential rain. Early that morning, General Smith's division of IV Corps took up positions astride the road from Yorktown in front of Fort Magruder and slightly to the right. Smith was waiting for orders from Brigadier General Edwin Sumner, temporarily detached from his II Corps to command the pursuit. At 65, Sumner was the oldest of the corps commanders; he had

served in the Army since 1819. Known to the troops as Bull, for his bellowing voice and brusque manner, Sumner was good at following orders but not very imaginative at formulating them.

While Sumner was trying to figure out what to do with Smith's division, a division of III Corps under Brigadier General Joseph Hooker marched up the road to Smith's left. Hooker was spoiling for a fight after the month-long siege of Yorktown, and he quickly took it upon himself to attack. At 7:30 a.m. he sent forward skirmishers to engage the Confederates in the rifle pits in front of Fort Magruder, and the battle was on.

Hooker called for artillery to soften up the enemy lines. The six cannon of Battery H, 1st U.S. Artillery, went into action. But soon Confederate artillery fire killed two officers and threw the artillerymen into confusion. This was the first taste of battle for most of these men, and some of them broke and ran.

Major Charles S. Wainwright, Hooker's Chief of Artillery, rode up to the guns and tried to rally the panicky men. "Though we slammed at them with our sabers and poked them out with the point, it was no good," he recalled. "Drive two or three to a gun and by the time you got some more up, the first had hid again."

Wainwright ordered the 6th New York Battery into position alongside Battery H. The New Yorkers, manning their own guns and those abandoned by the crews of Battery H, opened up a deadly fire. The cannonading rose in volume until, as a gunner recalled, "the air perfectly whistled, shrieked and hummed with the leaden storm."

Covered by the cannonading, Hooker's men went forward, and for two hours or so they made headway across the slashed clearing in front of the enemy redoubts. But Confederate strength was building. General Johnston, up beyond Williamsburg with the main body of his army, needed to delay the Federal attackers long enough to get his wagon trains out of their reach. He sent back to Fort Magruder Major General James Longstreet, a burly, stolid man who was the most dependable of his division commanders. By noon, Longstreet had committed his entire oversized division of six brigades; he counterattacked and began driving Hooker back. The 9th Alabama and the 19th Mississippi Regiments overran and captured both Federal batteries. The 12 guns were so deeply bogged down in the mud that the Confederates managed to extricate only four of them.

Longstreet was able to concentrate his troops against Hooker because the other Federal forces in the area were unaccountably idle. On Hooker's right, Sumner had not committed the bulk of Smith's division nor—with the exception of a single brigade—had he called up the two newly arrived Federal divisions that were milling around aimlessly in the immediate rear.

Hooker's regiments yielded only stubbornly; the general himself rode back and forth on his white horse shouting encouragement. Caught up in the retreat were men of Brigadier General John J. Peck's brigade of IV Corps, who had stumbled into the battle on Hooker's right and been swept back by the Confederate counterattack.

In places along the front, charging Confederates overran fleeing Federals, and gunfire gave way to hand-to-hand fighting. Seven Federal battle flags were captured in the melee. Smelling a rout, the Confederate cavalry commander, Brigadier General J.E.B. Stuart, ordered his men to ride in the wake of Longstreet's infantry, ready to pursue.

By about 4 p.m., the Federals had fallen back into the woods a good mile and a half from Fort Magruder. Just then, and just in time, help finally came.

In delivering it, General Sumner for some reason ignored the 8,000 idle troops on Hooker's right and the nearly 20,000 troops to the immediate rear; instead he ordered up Brigadier General Philip Kearny's division of III Corps. Though Kearny's outfit had been the last to leave Yorktown, the flamboyant one-armed general had been promoted from brigade to division commander only three days before, and he was in a hurry to prove his mettle in his new post. From miles back, he pushed his vanguard past road jams of thousands of Federal soldiers, threatening to burn their baggage trains if they did not get them off the road. To move faster, his men flung off their knapsacks by the side of the road.

Kearny's men reached the front at 4 p.m. Kearny himself—clenching the reins between his teeth and waving his saber with his good right arm—charged into the thick of the fighting, deliberately drawing enemy fire to expose the Confederate positions. Two of his staff officers were shot dead as they galloped behind him. After reconnoitering carefully to determine the enemy strength, Kearny launched his attack.

"Don't flinch, boys!" he shouted when some of his men hesitated. "They're shooting at me, not at you."

Everyone laughed, and the soldiers surged forward. Kearny was delighted with their high spirits. "That's it, boys!" he yelled. "That's it! Go in gaily!" Kearny personally led a charge by the 2nd Michigan Infantry that retook the captured Federal batteries.

Three Federal commanders confer during the Peninsular Campaign. Brigadier General Winfield Scott Hancock (*left*) and his division commander, Brigadier General William F. Smith (*center*), played prominent roles in the fighting at Williamsburg. Brigadier General John Newton commanded one of the two brigades that captured West Point, 35 miles from Richmond.

As Kearny's fresh troops gradually forced the Confederates back into the clearing in front of Fort Magruder and the redoubts to the left, an engagement took shape more than two miles to the north that would win the day for the Union. Sumner had not been entirely idle. After a morning reconnaissance had revealed two vacant redoubts at the northern end of the Confederate line, Sumner ordered a flanking move in that direction by about 2,500 men of Smith's division.

The brigade commander selected for the task was Brigadier General Winfield Scott Hancock, a 38-year-old West Point graduate. Hancock was tall, handsome and powerfully built, with a trumpet-like voice and an enormous repertoire of profanity.

Hancock led his men about two miles to the right, to a point near the York River. Then he crossed a narrow dam over a creek, and at noon seized the two unoccupied re-

doubts. He now held a strong position on a crest with woods on either flank. On the plain before him, he could see several other redoubts that appeared to be lightly defended. Beyond these works, in front of Fort Magruder, Hooker's and Kearny's men were hotly engaged. Hancock, in fact, was slightly to the rear of the fort, in position to cut Longstreet's line of retreat to Williamsburg.

Hancock unlimbered his light field artillery—10 three-inch ordnance rifles—and deployed a skirmish line. Before advancing farther, however, he needed reinforcements to protect his exposed right flank and rear. Twice he sent messengers to Sumner requesting help, and twice the old general refused him. Worse, at about 2 p.m., Sumner noted Hooker's deteriorating position on the Federal left and ordered Hancock to retire to the two empty redoubts he had taken two hours earlier.

Hancock stalled, dispatching additional messengers to Sumner in hopes that the general would change his mind. No help came, and shortly after 5 p.m. Hancock was finally preparing to retire as ordered when he saw a sudden flurry of Confederate activity on the plain in front of him.

At Fort Magruder, the Confederate commander, Longstreet, had finally taken notice of Hancock out on his left flank. Until Hancock's field artillery began hitting his position, Longstreet apparently had not even known about the undefended redoubts. The only general who had an intimate knowledge of the defenses was John Magruder, and he lay ill that day.

Longstreet now had in reserve a division under the command of Major General Daniel Harvey Hill, a cynical, strong-willed and extremely capable soldier. Hill and one of

Riding just behind the Federal color guard, Winfield Scott Hancock waves his men forward in the bayonet charge that routed the Confederates at Williamsburg. "This was one of the most brilliant engagements of the war," wrote McClellan, "and General Hancock merited the highest praise."

his brigade commanders, Brigadier General Jubal A. Early, were confident they could silence Hancock's artillery and requested permission to attack with 2,700 men. Longstreet doubted the wisdom of such an attack. He was fighting only to cover the withdrawal of the Confederate wagon trains past Williamsburg, and that outcome was now ensured. But the attack was finally approved by either Longstreet or Johnston (accounts differ), who had hurried back from beyond Williamsburg.

Hill and Early formed their line of four regiments. But almost immediately a confusion of commands sent the two flank regiments marching ahead prematurely while the other two regiments lagged behind. Thus disarrayed, the Confederates swarmed forward, screaming the Rebel yell and shouting "Bull Run!" and "Ball's Bluff!" They swiftly drove back Hancock's skirmishers.

Facing this ragged onslaught, Hancock calmly moved his infantry behind the crest of the ridge. The Confederates, exhilarated by the enemy's apparent retreat, swept ahead exultantly. As they closed to within 30 paces, Hancock's whole battle line stood up and opened fire.

Scores of Confederates were cut down by the first withering Federal volley. General Early, whose 24th Virginia suffered 189 losses that day, was himself shot in the shoulder as he urged his men onward; he was soon led away, faint from the loss of blood. And the Confederates kept falling; three successive color-bearers of the 5th North Carolina were shot down in a matter of moments. Then, as the Confederate assault buckled and stopped, Hancock galloped to the front. In a voice hoarse from shouting, he gave the

order that would make his reputation as a bold leader: "Forward! Charge!"

The Federal line swept forward. The Confederates fell back in rout, leaving behind 150 prisoners and a battle flag, which was proudly displayed by a young Federal staff lieutenant named George Armstrong Custer.

George McClellan had arrived in front of Fort Magruder just before the start of Hancock's engagement and had immediately sent up the reinforcements that Sumner had refused to commit. But reinforcements were no longer necessary. Hancock's engagement had ended in triumph. It had lasted precisely 23 minutes—"fierce, short and decisive," a Federal soldier wrote home.

McClellan was elated. "Hancock was superb," he wired Washington. The next morning, Tuesday, May 6, dawned bright and clear with McClellan ready to crush Fort Magruder from Hancock's reinforced position on the far right. The rain was gone, but so were the demoralized Confederates, who had resumed their retreat during the night. "Thousands of soldiers had sought shelter from the storm," General Hill recalled. "It was with the utmost difficulty that they could be driven out. Cold, tired, hungry, and jaded, many seemed indifferent alike to life or capture."

The unplanned Battle of Williamsburg had cost the Confederates 1,603 men killed, wounded and missing. The Federals had suffered higher casualties—a total of 2,239, including 456 dead.

But McClellan held the field; his giant army at last had a battle—and, more important, a victory—under its belt. Ahead of him beckoned the road to Richmond, now only 50 miles away.

A Prince's View of McClellan's Progress

As General George McClellan's army advanced in Virginia in 1862, its progress was traced in a series of lively watercolors, some of them shown here, by an artist who happened to be a member of the French Royal Family. He was François Ferdinand Philippe Louis Marie d'Orléans, the Prince de Joinville, who had gone into exile in England after the Revolution of 1848.

A staunch supporter of the Union cause, the Prince had joined McClellan's entourage as an observer in the autumn of 1861 and followed the army through the entire Peninsular Campaign. Then he returned to England, disappointed but not dismayed by McClellan's failure to win a decisive victory. Almost anything, he wrote, "can be done by the energy of a free people, battling for the right and for humanity."

General George McClellan dictates
an order in this watercolor by the
Prince de Joinville. A photograph of
McClellan with members of his staff
(*left*) shows the Prince de Joinville
(*second from right*) and his nephew,
the Comte de Paris (*far right*), who
served as an aide-de-camp.

In a spirited skirmish on February 7, 1862, Federal soldiers subdue Confederate snipers barricaded in a house near Vienna, Virginia. Captain Jacob P. Wilson of

the 5th Pennsylvania Cavalry, the officer who led the charge on the house, lies wounded beside his horse.

Federal soldiers at Manassas Junction survey the devastation that the Confederates left behind when they evacuated the town. In the wreckage, McClellan's men

Pursuing the Confederates who evacuated Centreville, Federal cavalrymen ford Bull Run. "We did not encounter the enemy anywhere," wrote the Prince de Joinville. "He had too great a head start on us."

found the charred hulks of a locomotive and freight cars, several smoldering storehouses, and hundreds of smashed barrels of flour, vinegar, molasses and meat.

Disembarking at Fort Monroe, Federal troops assemble for the march up the Peninsula to the Confederate stronghold of Yorktown. The Prince de Joinville wrote

"At times I counted several hundred vessels at the anchorage, among them 20 or 25 large steam transports waiting their turn to land the 15 or 20,000 men they brought."

At the siege of Yorktown, a Federal Zouave warns his comrades to take cover from a Confederate shell. The sight of the low-velocity rounds approaching from the distance gave the Federals time to duck, and the Prince de Joinville noted that shells would often "pass over the very place where spectators had been standing a moment before."

Federal work details apply the finishing touches to one of the batteries facing Yorktown. When the Confederates evacuated the town on May 3, just as McClellan was about to begin his bombardment, the Prince de Joinville noted ironically, "We had spent a whole month constructing gigantic works that have now become useless."

Victory within Reach

"We had a full and near view of the enemy and could almost see the white of their eyes. To miss was almost impossible. At every discharge numbers were seen to fall, and a constant stream of wounded, dying and dead was being borne rearward. Yet on they came, as resistless as an avalanche."

PRIVATE ROBERT R. RODDY, 85TH PENNSYLVANIA, WITH GENERAL CASEY'S DIVISION AT SEVEN PINES

5

While George McClellan prepared to move his enormous army toward Richmond from Williamsburg, a most unlikely field commander was about to open a second front in the Peninsular Campaign.

On Tuesday, May 6, President Lincoln arrived by ship at Fort Monroe. He was eager to find out at first hand what was taking McClellan so long—"to ascertain by personal observation," as his private secretaries later wrote, "whether some further vigilance and vigor might not be infused into the operations of the army and navy at that point."

In particular, the President was concerned about the Confederate ironclad *Virginia*, on the prowl again in Hampton Roads after a period in dry dock for repairs. The *Virginia's* presence not only menaced Federal shipping in the area but also prevented gunboats from steaming up the James River to protect the left flank of McClellan's army as it advanced on Richmond.

Lincoln also wanted to try out a plan proposed by Secretary of War Edwin Stanton, who had accompanied him on the journey along with Treasury Secretary Salmon Chase. The *Virginia's* home port of Norfolk, just across Hampton Roads from Fort Monroe, had been bypassed by McClellan; but, as Stanton pointed out, the evacuation of Yorktown had now left Norfolk glaringly exposed. With the help of the Federal Navy and the 10,000-man garrision at Fort Monroe, Lincoln and his companions intended to capture Norfolk and thereby deny the *Virginia* her base.

The man selected to lead the troops was the 78-year-old commander of Fort Monroe, Major General John E. Wool, who had begun his distinguished career fully half a century before, during the War of 1812. The years had not eroded Wool's military skills.

Lincoln, who was awkward even in his own environment, cut an outlandish figure on the deck of the flagship *Minnesota*. An officer wrote of him: "Dressed in a black suit with a very seedy crepe on his hat, and hanging over the railing, he looked like some hoosier just starting for home from California with store clothes and a boiled shirt on."

Lincoln's operation began with a false start. On May 8, he ordered a flotilla of Federal ships, led by the *Monitor*, to bombard the Confederate batteries on Sewell's Point, seven and a half miles north of Norfolk. Troops were embarked on transports for a landing there under cover of the bombardment. But before the transports could reach shore, the *Virginia* steamed up from Norfolk and took position off the target area. That ended the invasion at Sewell's Point.

A safer landing place was chosen to the east on Chesapeake Bay. The *Virginia* was unlikely to venture there. To do so she would have to negotiate the narrow channel between Fort Monroe and a tiny offshore bastion called Fort Wool, enduring a cross fire from big guns mounted on either side.

Emblazoned with Irish symbols, this bright green regimental banner identified the 37th New York, known as the Irish Rifles, whose color-bearers carried it with gallantry through the Peninsular Campaign.

To give the wreckers time, the mayor presented Wool and Chase with a set of rusty keys to the city. And he deliberately dragged out the surrender ceremonies, a witness remarked, "with all the formality of a medieval warden."

Despite the destruction of the navy yard, President Lincoln's operation was a glowing success, with at least one important consequence: The *Virginia*, standing offshore, was now a ship without a port—and without a future. Federal forts barred her way into Chesapeake Bay, and she drew too much water to make it up the James River to Richmond.

Late on the night of May 10, her captain, Josiah Tattnall, took the ironclad over to Craney Island, a couple of miles northwest of Norfolk. He gave the order to abandon ship and then set fire to a long fuse. At precisely 4:58 a.m., the 16-ton powder magazine exploded, destroying the pride of the Confederate Navy.

While Lincoln headed back to Washington on May 11, word of the *Virginia's* demise reached General McClellan at his camp near West Point at the head of the York River; the town had been taken on May 7 by Brigadier General William B. Franklin, whose division had steamed up the river ahead of the army in hopes of cutting off the retreating forces of General Johnston. At McClellan's urging, a flotilla of Federal warships, among them the *Monitor*, was now sent from Norfolk up the James River toward Richmond, about 70 miles away.

Thus, on two fronts, victory in the campaign lay within reach of the Union. The Confederates no longer had a warship capable of stopping the Federal gunboats on the

General Wool went ashore at the new site with 5,000 men on the night of May 9 to begin the march on Norfolk. Lincoln stayed behind to run things from Fort Monroe. The next morning the President experienced some of the frustrations common to commanders of even a small force. When one brigadier general seemed slow in reinforcing Wool, Lincoln lost his patience and said angrily, "Why are you here? Why not on the other side?" Then he slammed his stovepipe hat to the floor.

As it turned out, old General Wool did not need any help. He had landed without resistance and, on the next morning, accompanied by Salmon Chase, he marched up to the outskirts of Norfolk, where he was met by the mayor, William W. Lamb. The 9,000-man Confederate garrison under Major General Benjamin Huger already had evacuated the city, leaving behind a demolition crew to wreck the nearby Gosport Navy Yard.

James. And with Johnston falling back rapidly toward Richmond from the Peninsula, there seemed to be no formidable Confederate force between McClellan's 100,000-man army and the Confederate capital.

Panic gripped Richmond. The Virginia Legislature voted to burn the city rather than see it fall into enemy hands. Preparations were made to ship the Confederate archives to South Carolina. The Treasury gold was crated up, ready to be loaded aboard a train that was kept under steam.

Runaway soldiers and refugee families poured into Richmond from the Peninsula, doubling the city's prewar population of 40,000. Others fled the capital; among them were President Davis' wife, Varina, and their four children, whom he sent off to Raleigh, North Carolina. Some residents, concluding that the enemy was going to capture the city, set aside small quantities of tobacco to be used as currency in dealings with occupation troops.

On the 14th of May, Jefferson Davis called in his military adviser, General Robert E. Lee. The President and his Cabinet wanted to know the best line of defense south of Richmond if the government was forced to relinquish the capital. General Lee suggested the Staunton River, approximately 100 miles to the southwest. Then emotion broke through Lee's iron self-control. "But Richmond must not be given up," he exclaimed. "It shall not be given up!"

Though the gravest threat was McClellan's army, which was slowly marching over the muddy roads toward Richmond, the city was terrified by the more immediate danger posed by five Federal gunboats on the James. The squadron was now less than a day's journey from Richmond.

In the warships' path lay a single obstacle, and on it Lee pinned his immediate hope for the defense of the Confederate capital. Eight miles below Richmond, at a place called Drewry's Bluff, crews of soldiers, sailors and laborers under Lee's eldest son, Colonel Custis Lee, toiled feverishly to expand a set of existing defenses on the south bank of the river. The bluff, rising about 200 feet, commanded a sharp bend in the James—the last of the river's twists and turns before a straight stretch leading to Richmond.

About 300 yards downsteam from the foot of the bluff, Colonel Lee's men scuttled old ships and sank huge stone-filled cribs to form two lines of obstructions across the 120-yard-wide river.

Just upstream from the double line of obstructions, the wooden gunboat *Patrick Henry* took up station. At the foot of the bluff and on the far side of the river, sharpshooters who had recently evacuated Norfolk deployed in trenches. Sailors wrestled three heavy naval guns into place on the bluff to augment the three big columbiads—one 10-inch and two 8-inch—already there. All through the night of May 14, with the Federal gunboats only a few miles away, Lee's men worked in a drenching rain, digging rifle pits and filling sandbags.

The Confederates were ready when, at 7:35 a.m. the next morning, the Federal squadron came into view through the mist. When the lead ship, the newly commissioned ironclad *Galena*, reached a point 400 yards from the obstructions, the Confederate batteries on the bluff opened fire.

The *Galena* took two quick hits, but her captain and the leader of the squadron, Commander John Rodgers, held his fire. He calmly moved the *Galena* forward, and maneuvered her in the narrow channel so that her broadside could bear upon the bluff 600 yards distant. Then the *Galena* and the other Federal ships commenced firing. The roar of cannon—Federal and Confederate—shook windows in Richmond.

On the bluff, Confederate gunners were hard pressed. Fragments from 100-pound shells lobbed up by the *Galena* showered the gun emplacements, killing at least seven men. The 10-inch columbiad, accidentally loaded with a double charge of powder, recoiled off its platform. Nearby, a rain-soaked log casemate collapsed on its gun. And other Confederate guns had to cease firing temporarily to ration ammunition.

For all their problems, the Confederate gunners had a distinct advantage. They were able to pour plunging fire down on the *Galena*, penetrating the ironclad's thin deck armor repeatedly. The *Monitor*, attempting to relieve the *Galena*, moved forward at about 9 a.m., but from close in she could not elevate her two guns sufficiently to reach the high bluff. So she soon retired downstream.

Meanwhile, the wooden ships *Aroostook* and *Port Royal* and the little one-gun ironclad *Naugatuck* remained at anchor half a mile downstream. The crews did not dare to venture nearer, and in any case, they were preoccupied with the cross fire of musketry from Confederate sharpshooters entrenched on both banks of the river.

By 11 a.m., the *Galena* had taken about 50 hits. Her railings were shot away, her smokestack was riddled, and on her shattered decks lay 13 men dead and 11 wounded.

Commander Rodgers stood fast stubbornly until a shot from the *Patrick Henry* tore through the bow gun port, setting the *Galena* afire. At 11:05, after three and a half hours

Five Federal gunboats, heading up the James River to Richmond, are heavily damaged by Confederate fire from Drewry's Bluff. "It became evident," wrote an officer on the *Monitor (second from left)*, "that it was useless for us to contend against the terrific strength and accuracy of their fire."

of action, he gave the order to withdraw.

As the Federal squadron limped back down the James, the defenders of Drewry's Bluff cheered and hurled their caps into the air. Their gallant stand had staved off the waterborne threat to Richmond. The capital celebrated as well, though only briefly. Mc-Clellan's Army of the Potomac was now just 23 miles from Richmond and closing in.

But still only slowly. Indeed, McClellan was pursuing the Confederates so deliberately that General Kearny privately referred to him as the "Virginia creeper."

On May 10, McClellan and his army had begun pulling out of West Point. While one contingent moved overland, McClellan led another 15 miles west up the Pamunkey River, a tributary of the York, to a landing where the Richmond & York River Railroad crossed the Pamunkey. Here lay White House, the 4,000-acre plantation on which George Washington had courted the widow Martha Custis. Now the property belonged to the family of Robert E. Lee, whose wife was the granddaughter of Martha Custis Washington. By the 16th of May, most of the army was encamped along the Pamunkey between White House Landing and Cumberland Landing to the south.

McClellan posted a guard around the great house at the Lee plantation and established an enormous supply depot on the grounds. Scores of transports steamed up the York River and then the Pamunkey, bringing the 500 tons a day of supplies needed to sustain his army. Barges brought five locomotives and 80 rail cars, which McClellan had kept loaded and waiting in Baltimore harbor. The trains were to supply the troops as they marched west and to bring up McClellan's beloved siege guns.

In the midst of these preparations, McClellan got some encouraging news from Washington: His repeated requests for reinforcements were about to be rewarded. He had already been given one division of Irvin McDowell's I Corps, which had been withheld from the Peninsular Campaign in early April. Now he was to get the rest of McDowell's corps and additional troops under General James Shields. The reinforcements, adding up to about 40,000 men, had been stationed at Fredericksburg, midway between Richmond and Washington.

This welcome development contained an important and unwelcome catch, however. Though McClellan wanted McDowell's army to come by water, joining him at White House Landing, the President insisted that McDowell march south toward Richmond by the most direct route. As Lincoln saw it, the overland route would save time and also enable McDowell to stay between Washington and Johnston's Confederate army.

Whatever the merits of either route, Lincoln's decision forced McClellan to readjust his plan for taking Richmond. In preparation, he had reorganized his army into five

corps of two divisions each. He had intended to send the bulk of these forces due west along the railroad where it runs south of the Chickahominy River. But in order to join ranks with McDowell's southbound corps and cover his base at White House, McClellan had to extend his right wing. This he accomplished by deploying three corps—Sumner's II, Franklin's VI and Porter's V—in a northwesterly direction, so that they stretched from the railroad along the north bank of the curving Chickahominy for a distance of about 10 miles. On the extreme right, Porter's corps was drawn up in line near Mechanicsville, six miles northeast of Richmond.

South of the Chickahominy, meantime, McClellan deployed his left wing. Major General Erasmus D. Keyes's IV Corps proceeded westward along the Williamsburg Road and dug in near the crossroads called Seven Pines, six miles east of Richmond. Major General Samuel P. Heintzelman's III Corps was stationed five miles to Keyes's rear. By May 24, all the Federal dispositions were complete. The tips of both wings were so close to Richmond that the troops on the far left and far right could set their watches by the chimes of the capital's churches.

No sooner was every unit in place than McClellan learned from Washington that the deployment of his right wing was so much wasted effort. McDowell, scheduled to link up with McClellan just two days hence, was being diverted once again. As in early April, Lincoln was holding back McDowell because of the bold maneuvering of Confederate General Thomas J. Jackson up in the Shenandoah Valley west of Washington. This time, Lincoln and Stanton hoped to eliminate Jackson's threat to Washington by

Allan Pinkerton, detective for the Federal Army, sits smoking in the background *(left of tree)* at General McClellan's headquarters on the Peninsula. Though Pinkerton greatly exaggerated Confederate strength, he later boasted, "My system of obtaining knowledge was so thorough and complete, my sources of information were so varied, that there could be no serious mistake in the estimates."

trapping and destroying him with an envelopment by the forces of McDowell, Nathaniel Banks and John Frémont.

McDowell as well as McClellan protested this diversion of troops. THE REAL ISSUE, McClellan wired Stanton, IS IN THE BATTLE ABOUT TO BE FOUGHT IN FRONT OF RICHMOND. Indeed, Jackson was conducting his campaign expressly to prevent Federal forces from massing in even greater strength near Richmond.

Lincoln remained adamant; he was completely out of patience with McClellan's delays and his interminable demands for reinforcements. The President wired McClellan:

I THINK THE TIME IS NEAR WHEN YOU MUST EITHER ATTACK RICHMOND OR ELSE GIVE UP THE JOB AND COME TO THE DEFENSE OF WASHINGTON.

That was easier said than done, for Lincoln's various orders had left McClellan in an awkward position. He not only had lost McDowell's 40,000 men, but now found his army dangerously split, with three corps north of the Chickahominy River and two corps south of it.

This strange river was as quirky as its name (which some Federals pronounced as "Chicken-and-hominy"). In dry weather, the stream was sluggish and measured less

Soldiers of the 17th New York Volunteers *(right)* show their commanding officer, Colonel Henry S. Lansing *(center, arms akimbo),* a 12-pound howitzer they captured while routing Confederates near Hanover Court House.

than 15 yards wide over most of its course. But a slight rise in the river could quickly inundate the surrounding marshes and wooded bottom lands for as much as a mile. And the Chickahominy was currently on the rise; by late May it had reached its highest level in 20 years.

McClellan realized that the river threatened to cut communications between the two wings of his army, and he put his men to work building no fewer than 11 bridges across the river in a 12-mile stretch from Bottom's Bridge northwest to Mechanicsville. Though the narrow main channel of the river could be bridged with short spans, the waterlogged bottom lands on either side had to be overlaid with lengthy, elaborate corduroy approaches.

On May 27, while waiting for the completion of the bridges, McClellan extended his right flank even farther. Noting that the President's order had "simply suspended, not revoked" McDowell's march toward Richmond, McClellan still harbored hopes of soon seeing those 40,000 men marching down from Fredericksburg. To clear a path for them and to tear up the tracks of the Virginia Central Railroad, he sent a reinforced division commanded by General Fitz-John Porter to attack the Confederates at Hanover Court House, about 12 miles northwest of Mechanicsville.

There, with General Porter accompanying him, Brigadier General George W. Morell sent his brigade forward behind a screen of skirmishers from Colonel Hiram Berdan's Sharpshooters *(pages 100-101)*. Three batteries of artillery pounded Brigadier General Lawrence O'Bryan Branch's brigade of North Carolinians, who were concealed in the woods. Although outnumbered, Branch

impulsively launched an attack. One of Morell's regiments, the 25th New York, was broken, and a battery of artillery put out of action. But the Confederate charge was repulsed by the fresh 14th New York, whose fire was so intense that one officer reported his men had to pour water on their muskets to keep them cool enough to handle. Then Morell sent forward the "Irish 9th" Massachusetts and the 62nd Pennsylvania in a countercharge. "In a short time the retreat became a complete rout," wrote the colonel commanding the 14th New York. The Federals had lost 355 men dead and wounded to 200 for the Confederates, but they took 500 men prisoner.

To Joseph E. Johnston, the little battle at Hanover Court House was ominous, for McClellan's sudden move there strongly suggested an imminent linkup between his army and McDowell's. On that same day, another alarming report convinced Johnston that his suspicions were correct: McDowell's vanguard was seen marching south of Fredericksburg, only 25 miles from Porter at Hanover Court House.

Until now, Johnston's apparent lack of determination had bewildered President Davis and General Lee. Repeatedly refusing to tell them where or when he intended to make a stand, he had retreated to the south bank of the Chickahominy, the last natural defensive barrier before Richmond, just 12 miles away. Then, professing himself dissatisfied with the water supply there, he had fallen back to the outskirts of the capital.

Johnston's indecisiveness was, in truth, chronic. One of his acquaintances had noted that Johnston put off decision-making even on a bird-hunting expedition before the War. "He was a capital shot," said the man,

Troops of McClellan's army lounge on a hillside overlooking Cumberland Landing in this panoramic photo taken by James F. Gibson. From here, the immense Federal encampment extended two and a half miles north along the Pamunkey River to White House Landing.

"but with Colonel Johnston, the bird flew too high or too low, the dogs were too far or too near. Things never did suit him exactly. He was too fussy, too hard to please, too cautious, too much afraid to miss and risk his fine reputation for a crack shot. The exactly right time and place never came."

Yet Johnston was now persuaded that the right time and place had come. A linkup between McDowell and McClellan would provide the Federals with nearly 150,000 troops at the gates of Richmond—a superiority of better than 2 to 1. That eventuality had to be prevented at all cost.

Accordingly, Johnston devised a plan to strike the right wing of McClellan's divided army at Mechanicsville. The attack was set for May 29. But on the night of the 28th, in the midst of a war council with his generals, Johnston learned from a courier that McDowell's troops were not marching on Richmond after all, but returning to Fredericksburg. McDowell had made the demonstration south just to mislead Johnston.

Now that he did not have to worry about McDowell, Johnston switched to a plan he had preferred all along: He would attack south of the Chickahominy and overwhelm the Federal left wing—the two corps of Keyes and Heintzelman—before it could be reinforced from across the river.

A Confederate reconnaissance on May 30 showed that the Federal positions south of the river were unbalanced. The lead division under Brigadier General Silas Casey had deployed at right angles to the Williamsburg Road about a half mile west of the Seven Pines crossroads. His positions were reasonably strong on the left flank, which extended south of the road to the marshy border of White Oak Swamp, and they were heavily supported in the rear. There the divisions of Darius Couch and Philip Kearny were stacked up along the six-mile stretch of road between Seven Pines and Bottom's Bridge to the east, with Joseph Hooker's division deployed just to their south.

But the Federals were weak on the right. Confederate scouts had found that Casey's front extended north from the Williamsburg Road for a mile or so to Fair Oaks, a station on the Richmond & York River Railroad. And the Confederates had learned that the line was thinly manned. Northeast of Fair Oaks, a virtually impassable wilderness of marshes and dense woods stretched three miles to the Chickahominy River, where the nearest Federal reinforcements, Edwin Sumner's 17,000-man corps, were camped on the far bank.

Surveying all this, Johnston decided to attack in force (*map, page 140*) early the next day, May 31. In preparation, he divided his command in half, creating a left wing under Major General Gustavus W. Smith and a right wing under General Longstreet, each with three divisions. Smith would hold two of the left-wing divisions, Magruder's and A. P. Hill's, in reserve along the upper Chickahominy northeast of Richmond to prevent the crossing of the two Federal corps there. His third division, under Brigadier General W.H.C. Whiting, would support Longstreet to the south.

Longstreet's wing, three divisions totaling nearly 40,000 men, would make the main attack, striking east toward Seven Pines on three different routes. Major General Benjamin Huger would take the Charles City Road, which ran southeast from Richmond and intersected with a side road that led northward to Seven Pines. Daniel Harvey

Members of the Federal provost-marshal's staff enjoy a bit of relaxation in this portrait taken at Cumberland Landing. Among them were two future generals: Captain James W. Forsyth (*seated, far left*) and First Lieutenant George Armstrong Custer (*reclining at right*).

Hill was assigned to the Williamsburg Road, which ran due east from Richmond to Seven Pines. And Longstreet himself, supported by Whiting, would attack on the northern route. This was the Nine Mile Road, which ran roughly parallel to the Williamsburg Road for six miles, then cut southeastward, crossing the railroad at Fair Oaks station and—a mile beyond it—intersecting the Williamsburg Road at Seven Pines. Thus, the outnumbered Federal forces south of the Chickahominy would be hit on their left, on their front and on their vulnerable right.

The timing of the entire operation would depend on General Huger. When his lead brigade arrived at a predetermined position on the Charles City Road, about a mile and a half south of Seven Pines, Huger was to signal Hill, who would then launch his attack. On hearing the sound of Hill's musket fire, Longstreet, on the north, would throw his troops into action. Later, after making sure that the Confederate right flank was secure, Huger would be free to strike north for Seven Pines, where he would assist D. H. Hill.

It was a sound plan, and on the eve of the attack nature lent a helping hand. A violent rainstorm, which dumped more than three inches in the first two hours and continued into the night, turned the rising Chickahominy into a raging torrent that swamped several of McClellan's bridges and further isolated the targets of the impending Confederate attack.

At dawn on Saturday, May 31, under lowering clouds and on roads turned muddy by the night's rainstorm, Johnston's soldiers began the march eastward. Johnston was so secretive that he had not informed President Davis or General Lee of his plans, but with that many troops in motion practically every-

Bold to the point of recklessness, Confederate Major General Daniel Harvey Hill startled his troops in battle at Seven Pines by riding slowly through enemy fire smoking a cigar. "I saw that our men were wavering," Hill later explained, "and I wanted to give them confidence."

one in Richmond knew something was up. Expectant crowds gathered early on the hilltops of east Richmond in hopes of catching a glimpse of the battle that might determine the fate of their city.

The morning passed and no shots were heard. By noon, the thousands of spectators were growing impatient. As John B. Jones, a Confederate War Department clerk, noted in his diary, they were "venting their criticisms and anathemas like an audience at a theater when some accident or disarrangement behind the scenes prevents the curtain from rising."

The attack, scheduled for about 8 a.m., started late because the usually dependable James Longstreet was confused by his orders. To the other division commanders,

Johnston had sent specific written orders but not the overall plan. Only to Longstreet, who was entrusted with tactical command of the operation, did he give details of the entire plan—but not in writing. Though the two men talked for several hours on the eve of the attack, either Johnston did not make his intentions clear or Longstreet, who was slightly deaf, did not hear him.

As a result of what Johnston later mildly labeled a "misunderstanding," Longstreet marched his division south to the Williamsburg Road—the wrong road. This meant that Johnston's three-pronged assault now would be reduced to two. It also meant that the attack would be hours late in getting started, for in moving the wrong way Longstreet's six brigades had blocked the path of the division under Huger, who was key to launching the initial assault.

Only Hill's march went as planned. Advancing east on the Williamsburg Road, Hill stopped 1,000 yards from the Federal picket line and waited impatiently for the signal indicating that Huger had moved into place.

Hill had about 8,500 men in four brigades. They were deployed on either side of the road in thick woods and undergrowth. Visibility was so poor that Hill, anxious to prevent his troops from mistaking one another for the enemy, had each man wear a white strip of cloth around his hat.

At last, at about 1 p.m., Hill learned that Huger's lead brigade had come into position on the Charles City Road, five hours late. Immediately, Hill ordered the attack, and his men swarmed forward toward the enemy division under Silas Casey.

Casey's men were the greenest troops in the Army of the Potomac; his division was also understrength and poorly equipped—clearly the wrong outfit to put in a position as critical as Seven Pines. To make matters worse, Casey had failed to send out scouts or patrols. The Confederates surprised and easily broke his advance line, consisting of pickets and the 103rd Pennsylvania.

As the Confederates advanced, however, they ran into stiff resistance from Casey's main line of defense. The Federals were entrenched in a clearing behind an abatis. In the center of their quarter-mile-long earthworks was an unfinished, five-sided earthen fort, grandly known as Casey's Redoubt, which was defended by six pieces of artillery. For a time the line held.

The Confederates outnumbered the Federals nearly 2 to 1, and they used this advantage to the fullest. Brigadier General Robert Rodes led his troops against the front of Casey's Redoubt, and a brigade under General Gabriel Rains swept around to the right and rear of the little fort. Sharpshooters took up positions in trees at the fringe of White Oak Swamp and began picking off the gunners and their artillery horses inside the redoubt. General Hill personally led Captain Thomas H. Carter's battery of artillery to a position from which they could rake the redoubt. The commander of the Federal artillery in the fort was shot from his horse, and the defenders began to evacuate. Now the Confederates charged, screaming the Rebel yell. Threatened with encirclement and suffering casualties of nearly 40 per cent, Casey's men broke for the rear.

Casey tried desperately to rally them. An officer remembered seeing the general "raging among his retreating men, hatless, his white hair streaming in the wind." Another officer wrote: "Old Casey was as brave as a lion, and remained while his men would

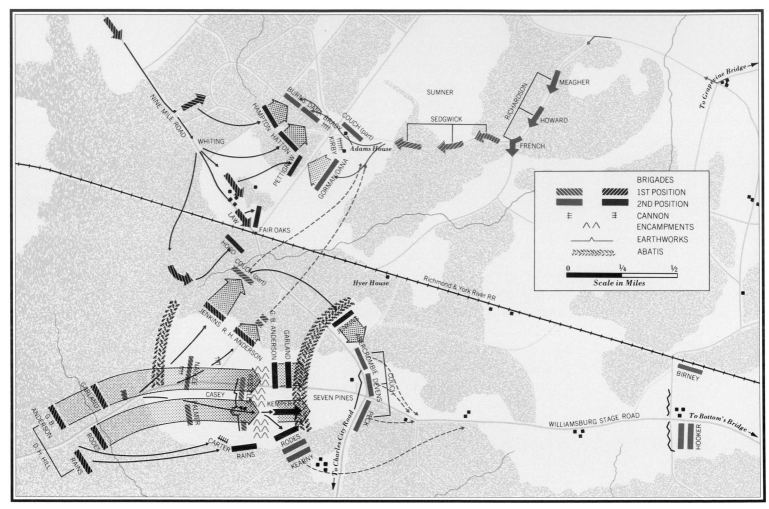

stand; he lost everything but the clothes he stood in.'' Casey's troops did not stop running until they reached Seven Pines.

As they came streaming back down the Williamsburg Road, General Keyes, commander of IV Corps, sent two of Darius Couch's regiments, the 55th New York and the 10th Massachusetts, forward to check the surging Confederates. The 55th was driven back and the 10th Massachusetts was nearly surrounded. ''It really seemed as though a man could not live there one moment,'' wrote a captain of the 10th. ''There was a perfect hissing in the air above and

around us, of grape and canister, shot and shell, railroad iron, bullet slugs and buckshot.'' Soon the Massachusetts men joined in the retreat.

By 3 p.m., though, the Federal battle lines had reformed at Seven Pines, and the going got tougher for Hill's attacking Confederates. They had fought without reinforcement for two hours, and now they faced a much larger force of Federal defenders. The remnants of Casey's division were buttressed by Couch's division and by two brigades of Philip Kearny's division.

Kearny had come rushing up from three

The Battle of Seven Pines, or Fair Oaks, began at 1 p.m. on May 31, when D. H. Hill's division launched a massive attack, overrunning Casey's Federal troops. The second Union line—Couch's division—then held at Seven Pines until flanked by Jenkins' regiments. At 5 p.m. Whiting's division began a series of unsuccessful attacks on reinforced Federal positions north of Fair Oaks.

miles back. He deployed his two brigades on the Federal left, south of the Williamsburg Road, and launched a flanking counterattack that carried almost to Casey's abandoned camp. "Another haphazard battle," Kearny wrote his wife the next day, "where I was sent for to redeem the blundering and short-comings of others." Again, as at the Battle of Williamsburg, the one-armed general seemed to lead a charmed life, galloping back and forth along the battle line, unscathed amid a hail of fire. He enjoyed himself immensely. When one of the colonels asked where to deploy his regiment, Kearny answered gaily, "Oh, anywhere! T'is all the same, Colonel, you'll find lovely fighting along the whole line."

The brunt of Kearny's counterattack was borne by Rodes's brigade. Rodes had counted on the support of Rains on his right, but Rains's troops had bogged down on the fringes of White Oak Swamp and failed to keep pace. It was tough enough for Rodes's Alabamians and Mississippians. They had to fight in swamp water hip-deep, propping their wounded against tree trunks to keep them from drowning.

Rodes himself took a nasty wound in the arm but remained in command for two more hours until pain and weakness forced him to retire. He gave the command to an energetic 30-year-old Georgian, Colonel John B. Gordon of the 6th Alabama. A businessman who had been trained in the law, Gordon had begun his military career only the year before when he was elected captain of a Georgia mountain company known as the Raccoon Roughs. His wife had followed him, and that afternoon she sat on a hilltop in Richmond a few miles away, listening to the fierce musketry—"pale and quiet, with clasped hands," said a companion, "statue-like, with her face toward the field of battle."

On that field, Gordon's horse was shot from under him and his coat nicked with bullets as he led the Alabamians on a charge through the abatis in front of Couch's division. His lieutenant colonel and major were both killed and his men fell on all sides. Gordon got a shock as he urged his troops forward. He wrote later, "I passed my young brother, only 19 years old, but captain of one of the companies. He had been shot through the lungs and was bleeding profusely. I did not stop; I could not stop, nor would he permit me to stop. There was no time for that— no time for anything except to move on and fire on." The 6th Alabama lost 59 per cent of its men, including 91 killed, the most for any Confederate regiment during a single action in the entire War.

While Gordon and others in D. H. Hill's division struggled to maintain their momentum, Hill sent an urgent plea for help to Longstreet, who remained in the rear. Longstreet, still confused about the battle plan, had misdirected four of his six brigades. He sent one brigade north to guard the railroad, though there were no Federals in that direction. Then he dispatched three more down the Charles City Road, where Benjamin Huger already had three idle brigades covering the southern flank.

At last, responding to Hill's calls for help, Longstreet put his two remaining brigades to good use. One under Colonel James L. Kemper marched up in support of John B. Gordon's mangled ranks on the Confederate right opposite Kearny.

As Kemper's men approached the battle, they came upon a demoralizing sight: "Long streams of wounded made their appearance

Troops of the 104th Pennsylvania launch a gallant counterattack at Fair Oaks. Holding his own banner aloft, color sergeant Hiram W. Purcell races forward in the face of advancing Confederates to rescue the flag of a fallen comrade.

on their way back to the rear, in every species of mutilation," wrote Private Alexander Hunter of the 17th Virginia. "Some were borne on stretchers, others swung in blankets from whose folds blood and gore dropped in horrible exudations, staining the ground and crimsoning the budding grass." Farther along, the troops of the 17th passed a wrecked Confederate battery whose gunners and horses all lay dead and wounded except for a little boy, the powder monkey, who had somehow escaped injury. Private Hunter remembered the boy: "He cowered behind a wheel of one of the guns, with eyes protruding, hands clasped, teeth clenched and a face wearing a look of horrified fright—face so white, so startling in its terror, that it haunted me for days after."

As Kemper's troops crossed the abandoned earthworks and charged through Casey's empty camp, they were caught in a murderous cross fire from artillery at the second line and from Kearny's brigades on their right flank. Hunter wrote, "The noise of the bullets ripping through the canvas of the tents added to the horrors of the day. Men screamed as the balls struck them down. The officers shouted out unmeaning cries. The flag went down. In five minutes 74 officers and men of the 17th Regiment fell." Kemper's troops, now disorganized and despairing, rushed rearward and dived into the empty Federal earthworks. They dared not retreat any farther, according to Hunter, "for to have attempted to run that gauntlet across the open field in our rear would have been to rattle dice with death."

Meantime, the other brigade that Longstreet committed was executing a bold maneuver. Starting out from the Williamsburg Road under Brigadier General Richard H.

Anderson, the brigade attacked northeastward on a dirt track, fighting nearly to the Nine Mile Road and splitting the Federal defense line between Fair Oaks and Seven Pines. Then, at about 4 p.m., Anderson assigned two of his regiments to Colonel Micah Jenkins, a gifted South Carolinian who, at the age of 26, had already shown bold leadership at Bull Run and Williamsburg.

Jenkins' men fought south to Seven Pines, then brashly cut east on the Williamsburg Road, slicing through the Federal center. General Couch, four of his regiments and an artillery battery were separated from the rest of the division and retreated north toward Fair Oaks. Jenkins wrote: "Pouring in my volleys at close range as I advanced, I drove them back, losing heavily myself, but killing

A Confederate hero for his bravery at Seven Pines, Colonel Micah Jenkins was already well known in his native South Carolina as an authority on military affairs. A year after graduating first in the class of 1854 at The Citadel, in Charleston, he established his own military academy in Yorkville, South Carolina.

numbers of the enemy, leaving the ground carpeted with dead and dying."

Not long before dusk, Jenkins smashed to a point half a mile east of Seven Pines. In the assault, 10 of the 11 South Carolinians in the color guard of the Palmetto Sharpshooters were cut down, but their battle flag never touched the ground. Kearny, who had been holding his own on the Federal left, was forced by Jenkins' bold thrust to fall back about a mile to protect his threatened flank.

Back on the Williamsburg Road, Longstreet, who still knew little about the progress of the battle, had decided around 4 p.m. that the right flank needed help, and sent Johnston a note requesting reinforcements. Though his attack was succeeding, Longstreet reported, his troops "were as sensitive about the flanks as a virgin."

On the Nine Mile Road, Johnston had spent much of the day in a muddle, not even aware that a battle was raging at Seven Pines. One of the few things Johnston did know was that Longstreet had taken the wrong road. He had sent out couriers that morning to look for his errant general, and after they found Longstreet on the Williamsburg Road about 10 a.m., Johnston despaired. "I wish all the troops were back in camp," he muttered.

Nonetheless, Johnston had still hoped to salvage his plan for a three-pronged attack. He decided to launch Whiting's division— the one originally earmarked as Longstreet's support—against Fair Oaks as soon as he heard firing from D. H. Hill's division on the Williamsburg Road. Before noon, Johnston moved Whiting's five brigades down the Nine Mile Road to a place called Old Tavern, two miles from Fair Oaks. Here, setting up

headquarters in a farmhouse, Johnston waited with Gustavus Smith and Whiting for the sound of Hill's musketry.

The hours passed. General Lee, who had ridden out from Richmond with President Davis, came up to the farmhouse and said he thought he had heard musket fire. No, Johnston assured him, it was just an artillery duel. For some reason—"some peculiar condition of the atmosphere," Johnston said later—he could not hear the heavy musketry scarcely two miles to the south. In another part of the house, staff officers heard it but, having not been told that it was a signal, did not realize its significance.

Not until Longstreet's call for reinforcements came shortly after 4 p.m. did Johnston realize what was happening. He wasted no time on recriminations, even though he was being asked to do what Longstreet was supposed to have done three hours before. He took personal command and started Whiting's division down the Nine Mile Road toward the battlefield, galloping away just as President Davis arrived at the farmhouse. If he saw Davis, Johnston made no effort to stop. He certainly did not want to listen to embarrassing questions about his mixed-up battle, and besides, he was in a hurry.

It was still not too late for Johnston to salvage a victory from the botched battle plan. Though he did not know it, Micah Jenkins' half brigade had split the Federal defenders at Seven Pines. If Johnston swooped down from the Confederate left with the 10,000 reinforcements of Whiting's division, he could link up with Jenkins to deliver a decisive blow. But in a day filled with unhappy accidents for Johnston, yet another frustration lay ahead on the Nine Mile Road.

Two of Thaddeus Lowe's mobile gas generators, with an apparatus for cooling and purifying the gas on the ground between them, stand ready to inflate the balloon

Thaddeus Lowe's All-seeing Balloons

In June 1861, the White House received a telegraph message from the balloon *Enterprise*, tethered 500 feet above the capital. THIS POINT OF OBSERVATION COMMANDS AN AREA NEARLY 50 MILES IN DIAMETER, reported the balloonist. THE CITY, WITH ITS GIRDLE OF ENCAMPMENTS, PRESENTS A SUPERB SCENE.

This feat by scientist-showman Thaddeus Lowe convinced the President of the value of an aeronautic corps. Despite opposition from convention-bound offi-

cers, the U.S. Balloon Corps was born.

Lowe was all things to his corps, including inventor of the devices that supported its operations. His most important invention was a gas generator to inflate balloons in the field; it was a wagonborne tank filled with water and iron filings that yielded hydrogen gas when doused with sulfuric acid. While previous balloons were tied to gas mains, Lowe's horse-drawn generators freed his balloons to move with the army.

Enterprise near the Capitol in June 1861. The inset shows the dashing Lowe at 30, roughly a year after he inaugurated his balloon service for the Federal Army.

Hurrying to inflate the *Intrepid* *(right)*, Lowe tests its gas pressure before ascending to report on a Confederate advance near Fair Oaks, Virginia, on June 1, 1862. To speed up the inflating, Lowe had cut out the bottom of a camp kettle and used it as a pipe to transfer gas into the *Intrepid* from a smaller balloon *(below)*.

Setting Up a Station in the Field

Thaddeus Lowe took three balloons to the Peninsula, each with a crew of 30 to 50 men to transport, operate and maintain it in the field. As the infantry established their lines in the field, the Balloon Corps set up their ground stations to the rear in level, sheltered clearings. The generators were then hitched up to inflate a balloon for flight. It took about three hours for tandem generators to inflate the largest balloon, the *Intrepid*, to its full dimensions—38 feet wide by 45 feet high. Then with the crew paying out the tethering ropes, the balloon rose to Lowe's preferred observation altitude, 300 feet, whence the aeronaut could see more than 15 miles around.

Thaddeus Lowe goes up in the *Intrepid* to observe the Battle of Fair Oaks as crewmen pay out the balloon's mooring ropes. "I ascended to the height desired," he wrote later, "and remained there, keeping the wires hot with information. As I reported the movements of the Confederates, the Union troops were maneuvering to offset their plans."

The barge *U.S.S. George Washington Parke Custis* and its tugboat tow one of Lowe's balloons up the James River. Formerly used to haul coal, the *Custis* was remodeled by Lowe to transport and launch a balloon. Thus it was the first vessel designed as an aircraft carrier.

Dawn Flights to Gather Intelligence

The best time for observation from a balloon was just before dawn, when the air was usually clear and campfires would reveal the positions of enemy troops. A change in the number of campfires between two predawn flights might bespeak troop movements, and this information could serve to deprive the enemy of the advantage of attacking by surprise. Such ascensions became routine.

To the Confederates, the aerial surveillance was a continual annoyance, one that compelled them to maintain elaborate concealment measures. "Even if the observer never saw anything," wrote one Confederate general, "his balloons would have been worth all they cost, trying to keep our movements out of sight."

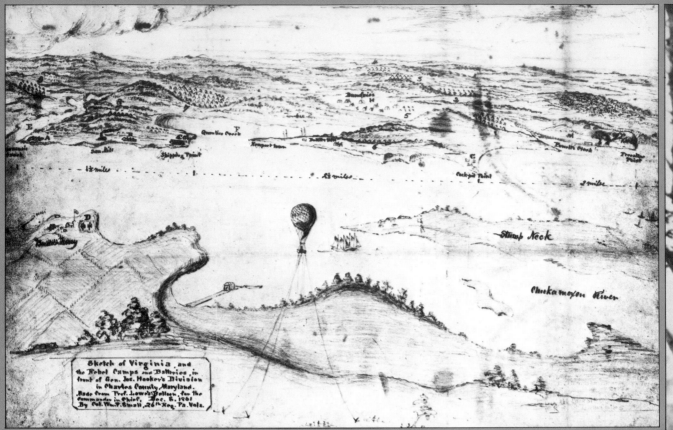

A panoramic map, sketched from 700 feet above the Maryland side of the lower Potomac, shows the Confederate dispositions on the Virginia side in December 1861. Letters and numbers refer to positions explained in an accompanying report.

Sending Word to the Troops

When Lowe's balloons operated from behind stable battle lines, intelligence gathering was a leisurely activity. Engineers made numerous aerial sketches for detailed scale maps, and observers wrote notes to be delivered later by messenger. But when speed was of the essence, as it was during major action on the Peninsula, the balloon observers would be linked with headquarters by telegraph. They could swiftly estimate the enemy's number and transmit the direction of his movements. And on occasion they became the eyes of the artillerymen. By noting the distance between shellbursts and target and then telegraphing corrections, the balloonists enabled gunners to hit enemy positions they could not see.

A telegraph operator relays intelligence from a Federal balloon station on the Peninsula as members of the ground crew anchor the balloon's mooring ropes.

Stalemate in the Swamp

"Seven Pines should have been a magnificent victory for us. It was really far from that, and while encouraging the soldiers in fighting and the belief in their ability to beat the enemy, it was a waste of life and a great disappointment."

MAJOR G. MOXLEY SORREL, C.S.A.

Rushing to save the battle, General Johnston led W.H.C. Whiting's troops to Fair Oaks shortly before 5 p.m. and found the place abandoned—the first encouraging sign that the general had seen all day. Now Seven Pines was only a mile away, and while Johnston was not sure of the situation there, he had at his disposal 10,000 fresh troops, enough to deliver a decisive blow.

But General Whiting suspected that Fair Oaks was not so deserted as it seemed. He had a hunch, he told Johnston, that the enemy was nearby in some strength on their left and rear, out in the impenetrable wilderness toward the Chickahominy where no Federal forces were supposed to be.

Johnston was impatient with that notion, and replied testily: "Oh, General Whiting, you are too cautious!" At that moment shells began to burst around them, pouring in from hidden artillery emplaced about 800 yards to the northeast—their left and rear. The Confederates dashed for cover.

The Federal attackers—four regiments and a battery of six guns—were fragments of Darius Couch's division. About an hour earlier, Micah Jenkins' flanking move had cut them off, Couch included, from the rest of the division. They made several attempts to fight their way back to their main force east of Seven Pines, but Couch gave it up as suicidal after two of his regimental commanders were killed.

Couch was leading the remnant up a path toward the Chickahominy when he spied Johnston's Confederates out on the Nine Mile Road. He hastily established a line of battle on either side of a building known as the Adams House. Thus posted on a rise facing west and commanding a marshy meadow that opened toward Fair Oaks, Couch ordered his gunners—Battery H of the 1st Pennsylvania Light Artillery, under Captain James Brady—to commence firing.

Whiting quickly responded, sending four regiments charging across the clearing toward the Adams House. Brady's 10-pounder Parrott guns repulsed them once, then again, but the third charge was the fiercest of all and threatened to overrun the battery. To his alarm Brady had run out of canister, the charge of lead balls so effective at close range. As a last resort he began firing regular explosive shells with the fuses set for point-blank range. The Confederates came within 20 yards of his cannon—and there the exploding shells blew them to pieces.

Nevertheless, Whiting's Confederates so far outnumbered Couch's handful that they would soon have overwhelmed the isolated Federal position had it not been for a remarkable turn of events. A long stream of blue-clad reinforcements suddenly appeared from an unexpected quarter—across the flooded Chickahominy.

Their arrival, shortly after 5 p.m., was the culmination of a daring trek that had begun four hours before on the north bank of the river. When the sounds of battle had first reached Federal headquarters at Gaines's

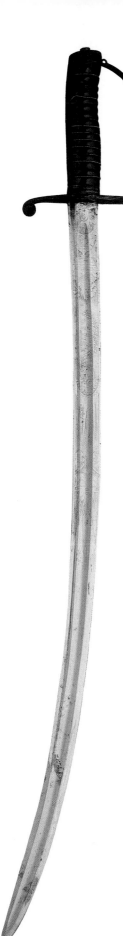

Mill, George McClellan, bedridden with malaria, sent an alert to General Edwin Sumner. McClellan's message merely warned Sumner's corps to be ready to move across the river toward Seven Pines. But the old general who had bungled at Williamsburg was taking no chances. He immediately marched his two divisions out of camp and down to two temporary bridges recently constructed over the Chickahominy. Then, when the order to move actually came from McClellan about 2:30 p.m., Sumner was ready to cross. But cross on what?

The Chickahominy, still rising from the previous day's violent storm, was on the rampage. The flooring of one bridge was under two feet of water; a single brigade managed to wade across, but then the span collapsed. A mile and a half downstream the other span, called Grapevine Bridge by the troops, looked hopeless as well. The rope that bound the log flooring had chafed apart and gaps now separated the logs; in the middle of the span the flooring threatened to float away.

As General Sumner neared the Grapevine Bridge, an engineer officer told him it would be impossible to cross. "Impossible?" thundered Sumner. "Sir, I tell you I *can* cross. I am ordered."

The men of Brigadier General John Sedgwick's 2nd Division surged forward. The bridge swayed, but the weight of the troops and their horse-drawn artillery settled the flooring back in place. The going was even harder on the far side of the bridge, where the logs of the corduroy approach drifted uselessly on the water covering a marsh 200 yards wide. The fieldpieces bogged down axle-deep and had to be unhitched and then wrestled to firm ground by infantrymen.

Undeterred, Sumner bulled ahead toward the sound of the gunfire. Two hours later he led his troops up to Couch's beleaguered regiments beside the Adams House. At the sight of reinforcements Couch felt, as he later wrote, that "God was with us and victory ours!"

The vanguard of Sumner's column, three of Sedgwick's brigades comprising about 8,000 troops, strengthened Couch's north-south defense line, then established a second line perpendicular to it. This new line extended west into the woods above the clearing so that it faced south. Thus the Federals were capable of pouring heavy cross fire on any Confederates who came into their murderous angle.

Johnston, out on the Nine Mile Road, did not realize yet that he was now facing a force equal in size to his own. Still thinking that he had to deal only with an isolated band of troublesome Federals before forging on to help Longstreet at Seven Pines, he had Whiting order three brigades to renew the attack against Couch's defenses.

Advancing across the meadow without artillery support, the Confederate troops took another severe pounding from the Federal guns. Brady's six cannon were now supplemented by five 12-pounder Napoleons of Battery I, 1st U.S. Artillery, commanded by 22-year-old First Lieutenant Edmund Kirby. The 11 guns poured out a steady stream of shell, spherical case, canister and solid shot. In a little more than two hours Brady and Kirby bombarded the enemy with no fewer than 500 rounds.

Some Confederates gallantly charged and managed to get within 15 yards of the Federal cannon before falling. Others entered the woods and blundered about haplessly in the devastating cross fire of musketry.

Two of the three Confederate brigade commanders were quickly put out of action. Brigadier General Robert Hatton, formerly a Congressman from Tennessee, was killed instantly as he led his troops into battle. Brigadier General James J. Pettigrew, a wealthy South Carolinian, was shot through the chest, left for dead and later captured. Brigadier General Wade Hampton, the 44-year-old South Carolina aristocrat who was reputed to be the largest landowner in the Confederacy, was hit in the foot. Hampton insisted on staying astride his horse while a surgeon removed the bullet. As the surgeon was dismounting to perform the operation, his own horse was shot from under him.

Toward dusk, Johnston finally realized what he was up against at Fair Oaks and reluctantly concluded that the battle would have to continue the next day. At about 7 p.m. he rode toward the front with his young orderly and a staff colonel, seeing to the disposition of his troops.

As they neared the edge of the battlefield, about 200 yards north of Fair Oaks, Johnston saw the officer duck his head as an enemy shell whistled by. Johnston smiled and said, "Colonel, there is no use of dodging; when you hear them they have passed."

Just then a Federal musket ball struck Johnston in the right shoulder. A moment later, a heavy fragment of shell from one of Lieutenant Kirby's guns slammed into the general's chest, knocking him to the ground unconscious.

As Johnston's orderly was dragging him from the field, President Davis and General Lee rode up. Davis rushed to the side of the general who had caused him so much grief

Hurrying to reinforce isolated Federal troops at Fair Oaks, men of General Edwin Sumner's corps tramp across a rickety, half-swamped footbridge spanning the flood-swollen Chickahominy River.

and asked if there was anything he could do. Johnston opened his eyes and shook his head. Then he realized that he had left behind his sword, which his father had used in the American Revolution. "I would not lose it for $10,000," Johnston said. "Will not someone please go back and get it for me?" He also asked that his missing brace of pistols be retrieved.

The stretcher-bearers waited while the fallen general's orderly retrieved the weapons from the battlefield, then they carried Johnston away. Back at Richmond, his recovery from broken ribs—and from the bleedings and purgings of the system that were then standard treatment—would require nearly six months.

With Johnston out of action, command fell upon the second-ranking officer, Major General Gustavus W. Smith. A large-framed, handsome man of 41 years, the Kentucky-born Smith had been a rising star in the prewar Army until he resigned in 1854 to take up a career as a civil engineer. He was serving as street commissioner of New York City when war broke out, and—being a pro-Southern Democrat—he had joined the Confederacy.

When Smith took over on the battlefield that Saturday night he faced mixed prospects. The advance of General Whiting's division had petered out into bloody stalemate at Fair Oaks. Farther south, however, the Confederates still appeared to have the upper hand. Generals James Longstreet and D. H. Hill had driven the Federals back to their third defense line, more than a mile east of Seven Pines, for a total Confederate gain of two and a half miles.

But at every point the Federal lines were

being strengthened. Sedgwick's division extended from the Chickahominy southward to Fair Oaks; a division under Brigadier General Israel B. Richardson, arriving from the north bank of the river, deployed along the railroad tracks from Fair Oaks eastward nearly a mile. At that point the Federal line turned south perpendicular to the Williamsburg Road; here it consisted of Philip Kearny's and Joseph Hooker's divisions, with the remnants of Couch's and Casey's divisions held in reserve. By dawn, the Federals' line was tight enough and strong enough to swing the balance of power in their favor, reversing the situation of the first day.

That evening, the exhausted troops of both sides slumped to the ground wherever darkness found them, in bog or woodland, and slept among the casualties. "It was a night of drizzling rain and inky darkness," a soldier in the 15th Massachusetts recalled. "All were wet to the hips, many had lost their shoes in the mud and the bodies of the dead and wounded were lying on every side. You could not move without falling over them—the air was filled with shrieks and groans."

It was an unnerving night for General Gustavus Smith, who was not only exhausted but apparently stunned by the sudden responsibility of overall command. Toward sundown Davis had asked what his plans were, and he had replied that he had none: He might have to withdraw, he said, or on the other hand he might be able to hold the ground won that day. Then Smith spent most of the night trying to decide what to do and finally selected a third alternative: to attack.

In the early-morning hours he summoned Longstreet and presented him with a battle plan that bore all the earmarks of expedi-

Confederate General Gustavus W. Smith, an officer of proven bravery, candidly discussed his breakdown under the responsibilities of overall command at Seven Pines. "I was completely prostrated by an attack of paralysis," he wrote; but 18 hours after he was relieved of command, "no symptom was manifested."

ence and confusion. While Whiting's battle-weary division would merely stand fast, pinning down the enemy troops to its front, Longstreet's entire right wing, three divisions, would wheel northward from their positions astride the Williamsburg Road and attack toward the railroad east of Fair Oaks.

Longstreet was cold to the idea. Perhaps he assumed that the Federals were being reinforced and that an attack would be futile and serve only to waste lives. He certainly knew that the terrain through which his men would have to advance was roadless, near-impenetrable woodland, impossible ground for an offensive. To Smith he voiced another concern: If his right wing attacked northward, its right flank would be nakedly vulnerable to a concerted Federal counterattack westward along the Williamsburg Road.

Smith blithely asserted that the Federals east of Seven Pines had been routed and then tried to mollify Longstreet by offering to call on the divisions of A. P. Hill and Magruder, guarding the Chickahominy, if they were needed. But Longstreet remained stubborn—indeed so stubborn that Smith had to order him to make the three-division attack. Longstreet rode off at 3 a.m., still grumbling but apparently compliant.

In fact, Longstreet had no intention of obeying Smith's order. His doubts about the battle plan aside, he had no respect for Smith's leadership and no confidence that Smith would back up his subordinates once the fighting started. "It was evident," Longstreet wrote later, "that our new commander would do nothing and we must look to accident for such aid as might be drawn to us during the battle."

Longstreet went to General D. H. Hill, who had set up headquarters in the bullet-riddled tent abandoned by Silas Casey, and told him to dispatch a few brigades to "develop" the enemy's front—that is, to probe the Federal positions to determine the size and strength of their forces. It was a far cry from the massive, three-division attack that Smith envisioned for the day to come.

As dawn broke, Smith was roused from a fitful sleep and handed a message from General Robert E. Lee. "It will be a glorious thing," Lee wrote, "if you gain a complete victory. Our success on the whole yesterday was good, but not complete." It is unlikely that Smith, in his agitated state, had much confidence in a Confederate victory of any degree. He would have had even less if knew of Longstreet's transgression.

At first light, D. H. Hill sent two of Longstreet's brigades under Brigadier Generals Cadmus M. Wilcox and Roger E. Pryor out on the Williamsburg Road to relieve Micah Jenkins and block any counterattack westward. Then he detached three brigades— one of Longstreet's under Brigadier General George E. Pickett and two of Huger's commanded by Brigadier Generals Lewis A. Armistead and William Mahone—and sent them north through the heavy woods toward the railroad.

Hill seemed as reluctant as Longstreet to engage the Federals. His instructions to the attacking brigade commanders were vague and incomplete. To Mahone, he merely said: "Take your brigade in there," and gestured toward the north. He neglected, moreover, to tell any of the three brigade commanders of the others' involvement in the advance; consequently each thought he was attacking alone and failed to maintain flank contact with the other two—a dangerous flaw that the Federals would exploit fully.

At 6:30 a.m. Mahone's troops and those of Armistead to the right collided with a Federal brigade under Brigadier General William H. French—the vanguard of Richardson's division, which was deployed along the railroad tracks. French, a stocky, florid-faced man who had a habit of blinking uncontrollably when excited (his men called him Old Blink-eye), had just ordered three of his four regiments into the woods south of the tracks to feel out the Confederates. A volley crashed into the Federals from 50 yards away and they came rushing back.

The din of musketry then grew deafening. An officer of the 57th New York recalled: "The firing rolled in long continuous volume, now slackening, now increasing, until it seemed as if pandemonium had broken loose and all the guns in the world were going off at once."

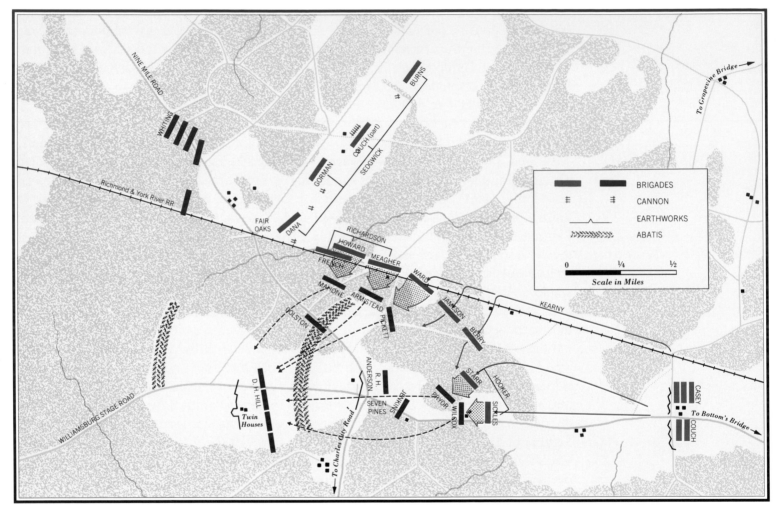

As French's troops took cover in the cut on the north side of the tracks, their excited commander supplied a touch of comic relief by tumbling into a deep hole full of muddy water. A captain shouted, "The general will be drowned!" The sheer absurdity of the notion—a general drowning in a mudhole while the air was thick with flying bullets—drew a huge roar of laughter from the ranks. French was more embarrassed than harmed. "His face grew redder than ever," an officer recalled. "He was pulled out, covered with mud and as mad as a March hare."

French nevertheless succeeded in stabiliz-

ing his line, and then he called for help from Brigadier General Oliver Otis Howard, whose brigade was deployed behind the railroad as the second line of Richardson's division. Howard, a pious New Englander who had distinguished himself at Bull Run, immediately sent the 81st Pennsylvania, under Colonel James Miller, across the railroad tracks and into the woods on French's far left to prevent a Confederate flank attack.

As the Pennsylvanians advanced, Miller detected activity ahead and then saw the shadowy outline of soldiers formed for battle. He quickly deployed his regiment for

At 6 a.m. on June 1, the second day of the Battle of Seven Pines, or Fair Oaks, D. H. Hill sent three brigades against Federal positions along the railroad north of Seven Pines. Troops from Richardson's and Kearny's divisions repulsed this Confederate threat, while Hooker's division counterattacked east of Seven Pines. The Confederates withdrew to their original positions, and the battle ended in stalemate.

fighting and barked out, "Ready, aim . . ." But before he could complete the command, one of his subordinates yelled, "Colonel! They are our own men!" Miller quickly ordered, "Recover arms!"

As his troops lowered their rifles, Miller called out to the strangers: "Who are you?" The answer came from a hundred throats—"Virginians!" They were from General Lewis Armistead's brigade, and they instantly unleashed a volley that killed Miller and scores of his men.

The 81st broke and scurried back toward the railroad, chased by the Virginians. At the sight of his men fleeing, General Howard sent his 22-year-old aide, First Lieutenant Nelson A. Miles, riding full tilt to rally them. Miles galloped through enemy fire that wounded his mount and grazed his ankle, turned the panicked Pennsylvanians around and soon had them firing at their enemy. For this display of gallantry, he was promoted to the rank of lieutenant colonel after the battle.

Howard then personally led the 61st and 64th New York through French's infantrymen and into the teeth of the Confederate fire. As he rode over the railroad tracks his horse was shot from under him, and he remounted a large gray commandeered by his aide and brother, First Lieutenant Charles Howard. The flashy gray made the general an even more conspicuous target as he rode just behind his skirmishers, and soon Howard was hit twice in quick succession, first in the right forearm by a small-caliber bullet and then in the elbow of the same arm by a .58-caliber Minié ball that shattered the joint. At almost the same instant the gray was hit and fell beneath him. In pain and shock, General Howard was led from the field by his brother, who was himself hit in the thigh minutes later.

(General Howard's tenacity cost him his right arm, a loss he suffered with aplomb and even humor. When General Kearny, who had lost his left arm, consoled him, saying, "I am sorry, General, but you must not mind it; the ladies will not think the less of you," Howard managed a laugh and replied, "There is one thing we can do, General—we can buy our gloves together!")

Shaken and confused by the loss of their brigade commander, the men of the 64th New York slowed down and then stopped, while to their right the 61st New York pushed on resolutely in the teeth of withering Confederate fire.

The 61st New York was commanded by a 26-year-old colonel named Francis Channing Barlow, a Harvard graduate and lawyer who was known for his toughness and temper. He added to that reputation as he led his men over the tracks and through French's line of battle. When some of his troops sprawled flat to escape a murderous volley from concealed Confederates, Barlow roared, "Who ordered you to lie down? Get up at once!" Then Barlow saw a group of terrified men crouching in the bushes and pointed them out to his troops as "examples of what a coward is."

Pushing fearlessly ahead in the thickets, Barlow came almost face to face with the Confederates of Mahone's brigade, and the fighting rose to fever pitch. "The singing of the balls was awful," Barlow reported. "Men were dying and groaning and running about with faces shot and arms shot, and it was an awful sight."

Some men perished in strange ways and postures. Sergeant Charles A. Fuller of Bar-

The 88th and 69th New York Volunteers cross railroad tracks to storm Confederate positions in the woods east of Fair Oaks. "The fire of the two regiments was s

telling," wrote their commander, Brigadier General Thomas F. Meagher, "that the enemy were compelled to retire, leaving their dead and wounded piled in the wood."

low's 61st New York saw a comrade live for a little while after he should have died. Wrote Fuller: "Sanford Brooks, a stalwart man of my company, and from my town, was shot through the head. The bullet entered at the side and just behind the eyes. The blow did not fell him to the ground—he stood upright with his gun clenched in one hand, his sightless eyes bulged out of his head and he staggered about, bereft of reason."

For all the carnage, Barlow and his men kept up their attack and edged forward. And for all their grit and fighting spirit, the Confederates under Mahone and Armistead gradually lost the upper hand. Mahone, a scrappy little man who weighed only 95 pounds, ordered repeated assaults on Richardson's positions, but his method was faulty. Instead of attacking with his full force, he committed his three regiments one at a time, and each was chewed up in turn by superior numbers. The 3rd Alabama was the first to charge; its commander, Colonel Tennent Lomax, was shot dead and the troops floundered about leaderless. In the chaos in front of the railroad track, 175 of the Alabamians were killed or wounded, and the fleeing survivors threw a scare into the next regiment to advance, the 12th Virginia. The 12th was repulsed, as was the 41st Virginia after it.

Finally, Mahone's brigade retreated all the way back to the main Confederate line along the Williamsburg Road. D. H. Hill, watching the retreat, was furious. He later blamed the Confederate shortcomings of the day entirely on Mahone.

On Mahone's right, Armistead's troops found the poor visibility in the dark woods at first a blessing and then a curse. It had enabled the Virginians to creep up on the 81st

Pennsylvania, then surprise and repulse the regiment. But later, as the fight grew hotter, the Confederates found that it was impossible to tell friend from foe. The 14th Virginia, mistaking troops to its front for the enemy, fired on the 53rd Virginia, throwing that regiment into confusion.

At about the same time, Armistead's men began to pay the price for Hill's haphazard preparation for the day's advance. Armistead made no attempt to maintain contact with the brigade to his right, under General George E. Pickett, because he did not know it was there; and Pickett had advanced with great deliberation, lagging far behind Armistead. A wide gap yawned between the two brigades, each of which thus had a flank exposed dangerously to the Federals.

Now Federal artillery and infantry began pouring fire into the Confederate gap. The barrage came from one of Kearny's brigades that had been deployed just down the tracks on the left of Richardson's division. Its commander, Colonel J. H. Hobart Ward, had encountered no significant Confederate opposition to his front, so he sidled along the tracks toward the sound of rifle fire—and ran right into Armistead's unprotected right flank. From the cover of the railroad cut, the Federals poured enfilading fire into Armistead's troops.

Then, sensing his advantage, Ward shouted, "Fire, charge, and give them the bayonet!" With a cheer the Federals leaped out of cover and stormed Armistead's flank. The Confederates crumbled before the onslaught and fled for the rear. Triumphant, Ward marched his men back to their stronghold on the tracks.

Pickett, in the meantime, still had not closed with the Federals, and he was sur-

The 71st New York Infantry of Brigadier General Daniel Sickles' Excelsior Brigade charges Confederate positions in a wood east of Seven Pines. The troops, wrote Sickles, "pushed forward at double-quick, and with a loud cheer charged into the timber, the enemy flying before them."

prised to hear the din of battle out beyond his left flank. He galloped off to investigate and saw scores of fugitives—Armistead's routed men—streaming toward the rear. "I could scarcely credit my own eyes in witnessing this misfortune on my left," Pickett wrote later. He rode farther until he found Armistead and a knot of officers trying in vain to restore order.

The two generals hastily conferred and then sent couriers galloping southward to ask for reinforcements from D. H. Hill. But none came—for reasons they would not learn until later. Fearing a concentrated Federal drive on their weakened position, Armistead and Pickett decided to pull back. As they withdrew, Richardson sent forward his third line, Brigadier General Thomas Francis Meagher's "Irish Brigade."

No Confederate commander seemed willing that morning to invest additional troops in what now bore all the earmarks of an abortive venture. Early in the day Longstreet had sent messages repeatedly to Gustavus Smith, demanding that he commit Whiting's division to the attack. But Smith must have realized that his orders were not being carried out—the volume of firing was not intense enough for a three-division assault—and, bewildered about what was happening, he hesitated and finally did nothing at all. Hill, for his part, had asked for reinforcements from Longstreet, but Longstreet chose not to respond. Sniffing a failure in the making, Longstreet was content to stand by and let events run their course.

Hill, realizing that he was entirely on his own, decided to give up the attack and at about 1 p.m. issued orders for his scattered brigades to pull back to the area around his headquarters, west of Seven Pines. Guarding the Williamsburg Road to the east, Generals Pryor and Wilcox were flabbergasted when they got the order to withdraw. All morning long their brigades had handily withstood attacks by Hooker's division, and as General Wilcox wrote later, "the men were eager for the fight, and everything seemed to indicate a success as full and complete as the day previous." Pryor and Wilcox nevertheless obeyed the order.

As they started their men rearward, Hooker seized the moment and sent his two brigades after the Confederates in a sweeping charge. At the same time, Ward, near the railroad, sent one of his regiments, the 40th New York, south; it came down like a bolt and sliced into the flank of Pryor's retreating troops. Led by a hot-tempered Irish colonel named Thomas Egan, five companies of the New Yorkers slashed through the Confederates all the way to the Williamsburg Road, losing 96 out of 231 men in the process. Every man of their color guard was killed or wounded. The regimental flag fell into the hands of Corporal Robert Greaves, who was severely wounded in the shoulder. Greaves carried the flag until the 40th New York's charge ended. Then he plunged the staff into the soft Peninsula soil as the Confederates retreated in the distance. Soon afterward, around 2 p.m., the firing sputtered to an inconclusive close. The battle was over.

It had been a mighty battle—the biggest and bloodiest thus far waged in the East. The Confederates, who called the engagement Seven Pines after the place of their success, suffered 6,134 casualties, including 980 dead. The Federals, having proved superior

at Fair Oaks, so named the battle. They had incurred 5,031 casualties, of whom 790 died.

On both sides, the soldiers had fought well, but what was most striking was the failure of command. McClellan spent the battle in bed and offered no leadership, except to send Sumner over the river to save the threatened corps. The ailing general's lapses were glaringly apparent to various subordinates, though the enlisted men still loved their "Little Mac." A disgruntled officer wrote: "McClellan appeared on the field shortly after the firing ceased and was received with as hearty cheers as if he had done the fighting. He did nothing, which will be judged good or bad according as one may think as to the propriety of vigorous action at that time."

On the Confederate side, Johnston and Longstreet had muffed their opportunity to destroy the Federal left wing, then tried later to make Benjamin Huger the scapegoat, blaming his inaction for their own failures. As for Gustavus Smith, he simply was not up to the burden of high command; two days after the battle he left the army, his nerves shattered.

So the great bloodletting had ended in stalemate. By dawn on June 2, the Confederates had withdrawn to the lines that existed before the fighting began, their backs against Richmond. Nor did the battle alter the Federal situation much, except that Sumner's corps was now south of the Chickahominy instead of north of it.

Johnston's counterthrust served to make the ever-careful McClellan even more cautious: He dug in deep, from White Oak Swamp to the Chickahominy, constructing elaborate defenses, bringing up more and more heavy guns and equipment for the intended siege of the Confederate capital. McClellan was confident that he had plenty of time—time to wait for McDowell's forces to join him, time to prepare meticulously for the siege. The Confederates, McClellan was certain, would remain in their earthworks before Richmond.

He was wrong: It was the Confederate Army that would strike first. The attack, falling at Mechanicsville only a few miles from the swampy battlegrounds of Seven Pines-Fair Oaks, would bring on a series of bitter engagements known as the Battles of the Seven Days.

Those battles marked the momentous debut of a bold new leader whose influence upon the course of the War was to be greater, perhaps, than that of any other general on either side. Jefferson Davis already had this officer in mind to serve as the permanent field commander in the East when Johnston was wounded at Seven Pines on May 31. On the following afternoon, Davis announced the name of the new commander. He was General Robert E. Lee.

Amid the carnage near Seven Pines, Federal troops do the grisly work of "burying the dead and burning the horses," as newspaper artist Alfred Waud captioned th

sketch. "The heat is perfectly awful," an officer wrote. "The dead decomposed yesterday, it was dreadful work to bury them."

PICTURE CREDITS

Credits from left to right are separated by semicolons, from top to bottom by dashes.

Cover: Painting by Rufus Zogbaum, courtesy N. S. Meyer Co., photographed by Al Freni. 2, 3: Map by Peter McGinn. 9: Painting by Alexander Lawrie, West Point Museum Collections, United States Military Academy, photographed by Henry Groskinsky. 10-13: Library of Congress. 14: From *The Armies of Europe* by George B. McClellan, published by J. B. Lippincott & Co., Philadelphia, 1861—from *Manual of Bayonet Exercises* by George B. McClellan, published by Lippincott, Grambo, and Co., Philadelphia, 1862. 15: U.S. Army Military History Institute, copied by Robert Walch. 18, 19: The Western Reserve Historical Society, Cleveland, Ohio. 20, 21: Prints Division, The New York Public Library, Astor, Lenox and Tilden Foundations. 22-25: Library of Congress. 26, 27: The New-York Historical Society. 28-31: Library of Congress. 32, 33: U.S. Army Military History Institute, copied by Robert Walch. 34-37: Library of Congress. 39: From the Special Collections Division, The University of Georgia Libraries. 40, 41: Painting by A. Wordsworth Thompson, White House Collection. 43: Valentine Museum, Richmond, Virginia. 44: Jon M. Nielson Collection. 45-49: Library of Congress. 50: U.S. Army Military History Institute, copied by Robert Walch. 51: Library of Congress. 52: Prints Division, The New York Public Library, Astor, Lenox and Tilden Foundations. 54, 55: Courtesy The Vermont Historical Society. 56, 57: Courtesy Old Salem, Inc., on loan by Wachovia Historical Society, photographed by Chip Henderson; courtesy Old Salem, Inc., copied by Chip Henderson—courtesy Old Salem, Inc., on loan by Ted C. Kerner, photographed by Chip Henderson. 58: Mississippi River Museum/Mud Island, Memphis, Tennessee, photographed by Murray Riss—courtesy Beverly DuBose, photographed by Kevin Youngblood—courtesy Troiani Collection, photographed by Al Freni. 59: Courtesy Ronn Palm—Museum of the Confederacy, photographed by Larry Sherer. 60: Milwaukee Public Museum, photographed by David Busch; courtesy Michael J. McAfee. 61: Museum of the City of Mobile, photographed by Larry Cantrell—courtesy Troiani Collection, photographed by Al Freni. 63: U.S. Army Military History Institute, copied by Robert Walch. 64, 65: Library of Congress. 66, 67: Courtesy The Vermont Historical Society. 69: Maryland Historical Society, Baltimore—U.S. Army Military History Institute/Dirk Salverian Collection. 70: Library of Congress. 71: National Archives, Neg. No. 111-B-3804. 72, 73: Courtesy The Western Reserve Historical Society, Cleveland, Ohio. 75: Library of Congress. 76, 77: Painting by Henry Bacon, West Point Museum Collections, United States Military Academy, photographed by Henry Groskinsky. 78: Library of Congress. 79: Cook Collection/Valentine Museum, Richmond, Virginia. 80, 81: Courtesy Bob McDonald. 82, 85: Library of Congress. 86, 87: U.S. Army Military History Institute, copied by Robert Walch. 88, 89: Library of Congress. 90, 91: Map by Walter Roberts. 92: Library of Congress. 94, 95: Yale University Art Gallery, gift of Samuel R. Betts. 96: National Archives. 98, 99: Courtesy The Vermont Historical Society. 100, 101: West Point Museum, photographed by Henry Groskinsky—U.S. Army Military History Institute, copied by Robert Walch; courtesy The Vermont Historical Society. 103: Courtesy The Vermont Historical Society. 104: Library of Congress. 106, 107: Courtesy The Vermont Historical Society. 108: Library of Congress; courtesy John W. Kuhl. 111: Courtesy The Vermont Historical Society. 112, 113: From *Battles of the Civil War 1861-1865: The Complete Kurz & Allison Prints*, published by Oxmoor House, Inc., Birmingham, Alabama, 1976. 114, 115: Library of Congress—courtesy Le Fondation Saint Louis, Paris, photographed by Dmitri Kessel. 116-123: Courtesy Le Fondation Saint Louis, Paris, photographed by Dmitri Kessel. 125: Courtesy State of New York, Division of Military and Naval Affairs, photographed by Henry Groskinsky. 126, 127: Library of Congress. 129: Department of the Navy/Naval Historical Center. 131: National Archives, Public Health Service Photo No. 90-CM-385. 132-137: Library of Congress. 138: Valentine Museum, Richmond, Virginia. 140: Map by Walter Roberts. 142, 143: Painting by William T. Trego, courtesy Bucks County Historical Society, photographed by Al Freni. 144: Courtesy Herb Peck Jr. 146, 147: National Archives, Neg. No. 16-AD-2; from *Above the Civil War* by Eugene Block, published by Howell-North Books, Berkeley, California, 1966. 148, 149: Library of Congress. 150, 151: Library of Congress; Prints Division, The New York Public Library, Astor, Lenox and Tilden Foundations. 152, 153: National Archives, Neg. No. 94-X-2; Brown Brothers. 155: Museum of the Confederacy, photographed by Larry Sherer. 156, 157: American Heritage Picture Collection. 158: Cook Collection/Valentine Museum, Richmond, Virginia. 160: Map by Walter Roberts. 162, 163: Courtesy Frank Wood, Alexandria, Virginia. 165: Library of Congress. 166: National Archives, Neg. No. 111-B-5125. 168, 169: Library of Congress.

ACKNOWLEDGMENTS

The editors thank the following individuals and institutions for their help in the preparation of this volume:
Connecticut: Stamford—Don Troiani. Waterbury—Frederick W. Chesson.
Kentucky: Fort Campbell—Stuart Vogt.
New York: Baldwin—Nick Picerno. Olivebridge—Seward R. Osborne. Oneonta—Huntington Library; James Milne Library, State University College at Oneonta.
Virginia: Alexandria—Kim B. Holien; Lloyd House, Alexandria Library. Falls Church—Christopher Nelson. Leesburg—John Divine. Richmond—William Mallory.

The index was prepared by Nicholas J. Anthony.

BIBLIOGRAPHY

Books

Andrews, J. Cutler, *The North Reports the Civil War.* University of Pittsburgh Press, 1955.

Arthur, Robert, *The Sieges of Yorktown: 1781 and 1862.* The Coast Artillery School, no date.

Averell, William Woods, *Ten Years in the Saddle: The Memoir of William Woods Averell.* Ed. by Edward J. Eckert and Nicholas J. Amato. Presidio Press, 1978.

Baquet, Camille, *History of the First Brigade, New Jersey Volunteers, from 1861 to 1865.* MacCrellish & Quigley, 1910.

Bellard, Alfred, *Gone for a Soldier: The Civil War Memoirs of Private Alfred Bellard.* Ed. by David Herbert Donald. Little, Brown and Company, 1975.

Beyer, W. F., and O. F. Keydel, eds., *Deeds of Valor,* Vol. 1. The Perrien-Keydel Company, 1906.

Bill, Alfred Hoyt, *The Beleaguered City: Richmond, 1861-1865.* Alfred A. Knopf, 1946.

Billings, John D., *Hardtack and Coffee, or the Unwritten Story of Army Life.* George M. Smith & Co., 1887.

Blair, Harry C., and Rebecca Tarshis, *Lincoln's Constant Ally: The Life of Colonel Edward D. Baker.* Oregon Historical Society, 1960.

Block, Eugene B., *Above the Civil War: The Story of Thaddeus Lowe, Balloonist, Inventor, Railway Builder.* Howell-North Books, 1966.

Boatner, Mark Mayo, III, *The Civil War Dictionary.* David McKay Company, Inc., 1959.

Bridges, Hal, *Lee's Maverick General: Daniel Harvey Hill.* McGraw-Hill Book Company, Inc., 1961.

Brown, J. Willard, *The Signal Corps, U.S.A., in the War of the Rebellion.* Arno Press, 1974.

Bruce, George Anson, *The Twentieth Regiment of Massachusetts Volunteer Infantry, 1861-1865.* Houghton, Mifflin and Company, 1906.

Bruce, Robert V., *Lincoln and the Tools of War.* The Bobbs-Merrill Company, Inc., 1956.

Buel, C. C., and Robert U. Johnson, eds., *Battles and Leaders of the Civil War,* Vols. 1 and 2. Castle Books, 1956.

Carter, Robert Goldthwaite, *Four Brothers in Blue, or Sunshine and Shadows of the War of the Rebellion: A Story of the Great Civil War from Bull Run to Appomattox.* University of Texas Press, 1978.

Catton, Bruce:
  Mr. Lincoln's Army. Doubleday & Company, Inc., 1951.
  Terrible Swift Sword (The Centennial History of the Civil War, Vol. 2). Doubleday & Company, 1963.
  This Hallowed Ground: The Story of the Union Side of the Civil War. Doubleday & Company, Inc., 1956.

Chase, Salmon P., *Inside Lincoln's Cabinet: The Civil War Diaries of Salmon P. Chase.* Ed. by David Donald. Longmans, Green and Co., 1954.

Clifford, Deborah Pickman, *Mine Eyes Have Seen the Glory: A Biography of Julia Ward Howe.* Little, Brown and Company, 1978.

Coggins, Jack, *Arms and Equipment of the Civil War.* The Fairfax Press, 1983.

Commager, Henry Steele, ed., *The Blue and the Gray: The Story of the Civil War as Told by Participants,* Vol. 1. New American Library, 1973.

Cooling, Benjamin Franklin, *Symbol, Sword, and Shield: Defending Washington during the Civil War.* Archon Books, 1975.

Cullen, Joseph P., *The Peninsula Campaign, 1862: McClellan & Lee Struggle for Richmond.* Bonanza Books, 1973.

Davenport, Alfred, *Camp and Field Life of the Fifth New York Volunteer Infantry.* Dick and Fitzgerald, 1879.

Dickey, Luther S., *History of the Eighty-fifth Regiment Pennsylvania Volunteer Infantry: 1861-1865.* J. C. & W. E. Powers, 1915.

Dowdey, Clifford, *The Seven Days: The Emergence of Robert E. Lee.* The Fairfax Press, 1964.

Edwards, William B., *Civil War Guns.* Castle Books, 1962.

Elliot, Charles Winslow, *Winfield Scott: The Soldier and the Man.* The Macmillan Company, 1937.

Esposito, Vincent J., ed., *The West Point Atlas of American Wars,* Vol. 1. Frederick A. Praeger, Publishers, 1959.

Favill, Josiah Marshall, *The Diary of a Young Officer Serving with the Armies of the United States during the War of the Rebellion.* R. R. Donnelley & Sons Company, 1909.

Foote, Shelby, *The Civil War, a Narrative: Fort Sumter to Perryville.* Random House, 1958.

Fox, William F., *Regimental Losses in the American Civil War, 1861-1865.* Albany Publishing Company, 1889.

Freeman, Douglas Southall, *Lee's Lieutenants: A Study in Command,* Vol. 1. Charles Scribner's Sons, 1942.

Frost, Lawrence A., *The Custer Album: A Pictorial Biography of General George A. Custer.* Superior Publishing Company, 1964.

Fuller, Charles A., *Personal Recollections of the War of 1861.* News Job Printing House, 1906.

Gibbon, John, *Personal Recollections of the Civil War.* Press of Morningside Bookshop, 1978.

Gordon, John B., *Reminiscences of the Civil War.* Charles Scribner's Sons, 1903.

Goss, Warren Lee, *Recollections of a Private: A Story of the Army of the Potomac.* Thomas Y. Crowell & Co., 1890.

Govan, Gilbert E., and James W. Livingood, *A Different Valor: The Story of General Joseph E. Johnston, C.S.A.* The Bobbs-Merrill Company, Inc., 1956.

Hassler, Warren W., Jr.:
  Commanders of the Army of the Potomac. Louisiana State University Press, 1962.
  General George B. McClellan: Shield of the Union. Louisiana State University Press, 1957.

Haydon, F. Stansbury, *Aeronautics in the Union and Confederate Armies,* Vol. 1. The Johns Hopkins Press, 1941.

Hebert, Walter H., *Fighting Joe Hooker.* The Bobbs-Merrill Company, 1944.

Hendrick, Burton J., *Lincoln's War Cabinet.* Peter Smith, 1965.

Holmes, Oliver Wendell, Jr., *Touched With Fire: Civil War Letters and Diary of Oliver Wendell Holmes, Jr., 1861-1864.* Ed. by Mark de Wolfe Howe. Harvard University Press, 1946.

Horan, James D., *The Pinkertons: The Detective Dynasty That Made History.* Crown Publishers, Inc., 1967.

Howard, Oliver Otis, *Autobiography of Oliver Otis Howard,* Vol. 1. The Baker & Taylor Company, 1907.

Hunter, Alexander, *Johnny Reb and Billy Yank.* The Neale Publishing Company, 1905.

Johnston, Joseph E., *Narrative of Military Operations Directed during the Late War Between the States.* Kraus Reprint, 1981.

Joinville, François Ferdinand Philippe Louise Marie d'Orléans, Prince de, *The Army of the Potomac: Its Organization, Its Commander, and Its Campaign.* Transl. by William Henry Hurlbert. Anson D. F. Randolph, 1862.

Kavaler, Lucy, *The Astors: A Family Chronicle of Pomp and Power.* Dodd, Mead & Company, 1966.

Kearny, Thomas, *General Philip Kearny: Battle Soldier of Five Wars.* G. P. Putnam's Sons, 1937.

Keeler, William Frederick, *Aboard the USS Monitor: 1862* (Naval Letters Series, Vol. 1). Ed. by Robert W. Daly. United States Naval Institute, 1964.

Lee, Richard M., *Mr. Lincoln's City: An Illustrated Guide to the Civil War Sites of Washington.* EPM Publications, Inc., 1981.

Leech, Margaret, *Reveille in Washington: 1860-1865.* Time-Life Books Inc., 1962.

Long, E. B., and Barbara Long, *The Civil War Day by Day: An Almanac, 1861-1865.* Doubleday & Company, Inc., 1971.

Longstreet, James, *From Manassas to Appomattox: Memoirs of the Civil War in America.* Indiana University Press, 1960.

Lonn, Ella, *Foreigners in the Union Army and Navy.* Greenwood Press, Publishers, 1951.

McAllister, Robert, *The Civil War Letters of General Robert McAllister.* Ed. by James I. Robertson Jr. Rutgers University Press, 1965.

McClellan, George B:
  McClellan's Own Story: The War for the Union. Charles L. Webster & Company, 1887.
  Manual of Bayonet Exercise: Prepared for the Use of the Army of the United States. J. B. Lippincott & Co., 1862.

Report on the Organization and Campaigns of the Army of the Potomac: To Which is Added an Account of the Campaign in Western Virginia. Sheldon & Company, Publishers, 1864.

Maurice, Frederick, *Statesmen and Soldiers of the Civil War: A Study of the Conduct of War.* Little, Brown and Company, 1926.

Michie, Peter S., *General McClellan.* D. Appleton and Company, 1915.

Miers, Earl Schenck, ed., *New Jersey and the Civil War: An Album of Contemporary Accounts* (The New Jersey Historical Series, Vol. 2). D. Van Nostrand Company, Inc., 1964.

Milbank, Jeremiah, Jr., *The First Century of Flight in America.* Princeton University Press, 1943.

Milton, George Fort, *Abraham Lincoln and the Fifth Column.* The Vanguard Press, 1942.

Myers, William Starr, *A Study in Personality: General George Brinton McClellan.* D. Appleton-Century Company, 1934.

Nevins, Allan, *The War for the Union,* Vols. 1 and 2. Charles Scribner's Sons, 1959, 1960.

Oates, Stephen B., *With Malice toward None: The Life of Abraham Lincoln.* Harper & Row, Publishers, 1977.

Olson, Kenneth E., *Music and Musket: Bands and Bandsmen of the American Civil War.* Greenwood Press, 1981.

Paris, Louise Philippe Albert d'Orléans, Comte de, *History of the Civil War in America,* Vol. 1. Jos. H. Coates & Co., 1875.

Patch, Joseph Dorst, *The Battle of Ball's Bluff.* Potomac Press, 1958.

Peterson, Harold L., *Round Shot and Rammers.* Bonanza Books, 1969.

Randall, J. G., *Lincoln the President: Springfield to Gettysburg.* Peter Smith, 1976.

Reed, Rowena, *Combined Operations in the Civil War.* Naval Institute Press, 1978.

Reminisco, Don Pedro Quaerendo, *Life in the Union Army; or, Notings and Reminiscences of a Two Years' Volunteer.* Sinclair Tousey, 1864.

Roe, Alfred S., *The Tenth Regiment Massachusetts Volunteer Infantry: 1861-1864.* Tenth Regiment Veteran Association, 1909.

Ropes, John Codman, *The Story of the Civil War,* Part 1. G. P. Putnam's Sons, 1894.

Sandburg, Carl, *Abraham Lincoln: The War Years.* Harcourt, Brace & Company, 1939.

Smith, Gustavus W., *The Battle of Seven Pines.* C. G. Crawford, Printer and Stationer, 1891.

Sorrel, Gilbert Moxley, *Recollections of a Confederate Staff Officer.* Ed. by Bell Irvin Wiley. McCowat-Mercer Press, 1958.

Starr, Louis M., *Bohemian Brigade: Civil War Newsmen in Action.* Alfred A. Knopf, 1954.

Stevens, C. A., *Berdan's United States Sharpshooters in the Army of the Potomac: 1861-1865.* The Price-McGill Company, 1892.

Strode, Hudson, *Jefferson Davis: Confederate President.* Harcourt, Brace and Company, 1959.

Swinton, William, *Campaigns of the Army of the Potomac.* Charles Scribner's Sons, 1882.

Thomas, Benjamin P., *Abraham Lincoln.* Alfred A. Knopf, 1952.

Thomas, Benjamin P., and Harold M. Hyman, *Stanton: The Life and Times of Lincoln's Secretary of War.* Alfred A. Knopf, 1962.

Thomas, Howard, *Boys in Blue from the Adirondack Foothills.* Prospect Books, 1960.

Thomas, John P., *Career and Character of General Micah Jenkins, C.S.A.* The State Company, 1903.

Todd, Frederick P., *American Military Equipage: 1851-1872.* Charles Scribner's Sons, 1978.

Todd, William, *The Seventy-ninth Highlanders: New York Volunteers in the War of Rebellion, 1861-1865.* Press of Brandow, Barton & Co., 1886.

Tucker, Glenn, *Hancock the Superb.* Bobbs-Merrill Company, Inc., 1960.

Turner, George Edgar, *Victory Rode the Rails: The Strategic Place of the Railroads in the Civil War.* The Bobbs-Merrill Company, Inc., 1953.

United States Congress Joint Committee on the Conduct of the War, *The Battle of Ball's Bluff.* Kraus Reprint Co., 1977.

United States Navy, *Official Records of the Union and Confederate Navies in the War of the Rebellion.* Government Printing Office, 1898.

United States War Department:
Revised Regulations for the Army of the United States, 1861. Civil War Times Illustrated, 1974.
The War of the Rebellion: A Compilation of the Official Records of the Union and Confederate Armies. Government Printing Office, 1902.

Vandiver, Frank E., *Rebel Brass: The Confederate Command System.* Greenwood Press, Publishers, 1969.

Wainwright, Charles S., *A Diary of Battle: The Personal Journals of Colonel Charles S. Wainwright, 1861-1865.* Ed. by Allan Nevins. Harcourt, Brace & World, Inc., 1962.

Warner, Ezra J.:
Generals in Blue: Lives of the Union Commanders. Louisiana State University Press, 1964.
Generals in Gray: Lives of the Confederate Commanders. Louisiana State University Press, 1959.

Webb, Alexander S., *The Peninsula: McClellan's Campaign of 1862.* Jack Brussel, Publisher, no date.

Weld, Stephen Minot, *War Diary and Letters of Stephen Minot Weld, 1861-1865.* Massachusetts Historical Society, 1979.

Werstein, Irving:
Abraham Lincoln versus Jefferson Davis. Thomas Y. Crowell Company, 1959.
Kearny the Magnificent: The Story of General Philip Kearny, 1815-1862. The John Day Company, 1962.

Wiley, Bell Irvin, *The Life of Billy Yank: The Common Soldier of the Union.* Louisiana State University Press, 1978.

Williams, Kenneth P., *Lincoln Finds a General: A Military Study of the Civil War,* Vol. 1. The Macmillan Company, 1949.

Williams, T. Harry:
Lincoln and His Generals. Vintage Books, 1952.
Lincoln and the Radicals. The University of Wisconsin Press, 1941.

Wise, Jennings Cropper, *The Long Arm of Lee: The History of the Artillery of the Army of Northern Virginia.* Oxford University Press, 1959.

Wistar, Issac Jones, *Autobiography of Issac Jones Wistar: 1827-1905.* The Wistar Institute of Anatomy and Biology, 1937.

Other Sources

Lowe, T.S.C., "Observation Balloons in the Battle of Fair Oaks," *Review of Reviews,* February 1911.

Newsom, Jon, "The American Brass Band Movement," *The Quarterly Journal of the Library of Congress,* Spring 1979.

"The Peninsular Campaign of General McClellan in 1862," Papers Read before the Military Historical Society of Massachusetts in 1876, 1877, 1878 and 1880, John R. Osgood and Company, 1881.

"Stories of Our Soldiers: War Reminiscences, by 'Carleton' and by Soldiers of New England," The Journal Newspaper Company, 1893.

Wiley, Bell I., "The Common Soldier of the Civil War," *Civil War Times Illustrated,* 1973.

INDEX